DATE DUE

WILLIAM SAROYAN

An Armenian Trilogy

Edited with an

Introductory Essay and Glossary

by

Dickran Kouymjian

The Press
at
California State University, Fresno
Fresno, California 93740

CONTENTS

PS 3537 .A826 A75 1986

Saroyan, William, 1908–

An Armenian trilogy

Printed in U.S.A.

Copy Editor: Carla Jean Millar
Production Supervisor: Rosie Gutierrez

LC #86-61823
Armenians, Bitlis, Haratch, Copyright © 1986
by the Willliam Saroyan Foundation

Preface, Introduction, Glossary, Copyright © 1986
by Dickran Kouymjian

To William Saroyan

May thy will be done.

PREFACE

William Saroyan's public voice has been known and loved for fifty years by a succession of readers and theatergoers who have enjoyed in his work their sparkle and humor, their challenge to upper-class and establishment values, and their insistence that the common man is a dignified subject of art. Yet like everyone, Saroyan, too, had an inner, non-public world, and in this book he speaks in one of his private voices. The most important elements of this interior landscape were *family*, grandmother, mother, and especially his father; *origins*, his Armenian experience; and *self*, his struggle to define, understand, and accept the person he had become. We know very little about his private thoughts beyond those he shared voluntarily with us as readers.

The plays brought together here are concerned with Saroyan's Armenian heritage. Though they are intense, they are probably no more so than other works of his that are preoccupied with family and self—his journals, for instance. Nor were they necessarily more important to him personally, nor more useful for our understanding of his priorities than his public works, especially those dealing with universal human traits of being. Though the plays in this volume are the first of his unpublished manuscripts to be issued, one should not attach to them a greater value for constructing Saroyan's literary history than other unpublished or already published plays, novels, stories, and auto-biographies. Nevertheless, in these plays Saroyan proclaims the impact of an Armenian background on his philosophical world-view, inviting critics and scholars to refocus their attention on this dimension of his creation. Like all of Saroyan's writing, these dialogues from Armenian life in exile are intended to provoke as they entertain.

Saroyan wanted the plays to be studied and published; that is why he passed them on to me for use in my classes. In his final years he became more attached to California State University, Fresno—the only university in Fresno County and the surrounding area—and particularly to its Armenian Studies Program. In 1980 he asked me to arrange a meeting with the new president of the university, Dr. Harold Haak, and the chairman of the University Foundation, the late Leon Peters, to discuss the disposition of his papers and witness the signing of a new will. In his will he designated Fresno State, along with the Bancroft Library at the University of California, Berkeley, as repositories of the literary estate he bequeathed to the William Saroyan Foundation for proper management and study. It is fitting that the first of a long series of unpublished works directly addresses his own Armenian environment and in part the Fresno of his youth. It is also appropriate that they be published by the Press at California State University, Fresno.

In editing Saroyan's manuscripts, I have followed as closely as possible his own practices when transforming typescript to printed page: correcting typing mistakes (whether omissions or misstrikes), eliminating unintentional repetitions, making consistent the spelling of foreign, especially Armenian, names and terms, and dividing the plays into appropriate acts. Saroyan himself edited one of the three works, *Armenians*, before sending it to New York for performance. As usual his changes were written directly on the acting script and were of three kinds: minor deletions, minor additions, underlining for emphasis. The final version remains essentially the same as the first and only drafts. Had he edited *Bitlis* and *Haratch* for production or publication, I believe the changes would have been equally insignificant. I do not believe it wise to outguess an author about his own work. In editing the latter two plays, though I have not made minor deletions or additions, and even with the lapse of time, I believe they are published in this volume as Saroyan would have wanted them to be.

I would like to thank the William Saroyan Foundation and its Executive Chairman, Robert Setrakian, for agreeing to the publication of these plays, thereby strengthening the ties between Saroyan and Fresno and its University.

A number of people have responded to my requests for details on certain points and characters in the plays or for unpublished manuscripts. I have the pleasure of thanking them publicly: Arpik Missakian, editor of *Haratch*, Paris; Séta Kapoïan of Paris; Margaret J. Dadian of Washington, D.C.; Allison Moore of the Bancroft Library, Berkeley; Dr. James D. Hart, Director of the Bancroft Library; Professor Leo Hamalian of City College of New York; Professor Khachig Tölölyan of Wesleyan University, Middletown, Connecticut; Dr. Sarkis Karayan of Newbury Park, California; Barlow Der Mugrdechian of California State University, Fresno; Edward Setrakian of New York City; Bedros Zobian (Zobyan), of Don Mills, Ontario, Canada; I would also like to thank Carla Millar and Rosie Gutierrez for their care with the technical aspects of the book, and finally, Joseph Satin, Director of the Press at California State University, Fresno and Kenneth Seib, Senior Editor, for their help and encouragement.

Dickran Kouymjian
Paris, July 4, 1985

INTRODUCTION

The works in this volume are the first to be made available from
the unpublished legacy left by William Saroyan. For a decade, from
the mid-1930s to the 1940s, he was one of the world's best known
writers, a pivotal force in American letters. During his lifetime, Saroyan
transformed his immense creative energy into more than fifty volumes.
Curiously comfortable in almost every genre, an unusual quality for
an American writer, Saroyan distributed his efforts nearly equally
among collections of stories, plays, novels, and autobiographical
reflections. Yet, concealed behind this impressive published output,
there was, according to the author's frequent assertion, just as much
unpublished writing waiting to be discovered. This trilogy represents
the beginning of the Saroyan legacy.

As a writer and personality, who cultivated attention in the first
half of his career in order to avoid it in the last half, Saroyan always
attracted a loyal group of readers and admirers. How else is one to
explain that in the four years since his death, eleven volumes have
been devoted to him: four of his own works, including the final memoir
Births, five critical or biographical studies, and two special issues of
literary quarterlies?

Hundreds of manuscripts remain unpublished, including drama,
fiction, journals, diaries, dreambooks, and a voluminous and fetching

correspondence. If individually their value does not surpass his most acclaimed works, neither does it fall below them. Saroyan often said that all his writing was done by the same person in the same way; he seldom recognized one work as being better than another.

The three plays offered here were written during the last ten years of William Saroyan's career, and they address a special concern of the writer: his ethnic origin. Their order is based on the progressive earnestness with which they treat the problem of being forced to live in exile. During Saroyan's lifetime little was said about the effect of national background on his writing; scant attention was given to his sensitivity to it, even though it is manifest in the earlier stories and later memoirs. Intimately familiar with the richness and foibles of one particular minority, he used the Armenians to show that behind the often unique peculiarities of any one nation there resides a universal humanity.

In these plays, by using exclusively Armenian characters engaged in conflicts special to them, Saroyan went beyond the marginal or indirect treatment of ethnicity found in many of his first stories, even those of *My Name Is Aram*, in which problems experienced because of nationality seem incidental compared to broader human questions. Central to these plays is the Armenian diaspora: the separation from native land, birthplace, home, and nation. Through an often profound discussion of the particularities of the dilemma he inherited by the accident of his Armenian birth, Saroyan examines the universal pain and paradox of the exile in a world where not only Armenian, Jew, and Gypsy, but Cambodian, Vietnamese, Palestinian, and Pole are synonyms for refugee and alien.

In semi-exile in Paris after 1959, but firmly rerooted in Fresno, California, his birthplace, from 1963 on, Saroyan, in search of an autobiography, wrote one work after another about his remembered past. Ten books appeared in a score of years, garnished with a continuous seasoning of stories and three volumes of plays: *Sam, the Highest Jumper of Them All, or The London Comedy* (1961), *The Dogs, or The Paris Comedy and Two Other Plays* (1969), *Assassinations and Jim, Sam and Anna* (1979).

In spite of the prolific publication of memoirs, often slices from his profuse journals (a month here, a month there), playwriting occupied him at least as much. In later years, Saroyan regarded theater as a more direct vehicle for communicating ideas and reflections than story or essay. It was the immediacy of speech that appealed to him. He was always considered a master of dialogue, and those who spent time with him knew he was a remarkable and overwhelming talker.

Not surprisingly, Saroyan regularly wrote plays, often several at the same time, always rapidly and in quantities that threaten credulity; for example he wrote more than fifteen in the spring and summer of 1975. They are all unknown. He submitted few for publication or performance, nor did he circulate them among close friends; instead, he carefully preserved them for their future resurrection.

The long letter addressed to the fifteen critics who panned his *Sam, the Highest Jumper of Them All*, (printed in the introduction to the edition), underscores Saroyan's constant disappointment with those who failed to understand his plays. "I write plays and you write criticism. . . . There are fifteen of you and one of me. I say Sam is a good play. I am sorry you say it isn't. One of us is obviously mistaken. Knowing the paltry little I know, I cannot believe it is me." While discouraged by the judgment of critics supposedly able to discern originality and seriousness of purpose, Saroyan was encouraged during the 1950s and 60s by European playwrights who used surrealistic, existential, and absurdist techniques similar to those he had used two decades earlier. Saroyan wrote his plays for posterity, as he said many times, perhaps nowhere more concisely than in a letter of March 7, 1975, to Gerald Pollinger, his London agent:

> I write at least one new large play a year and quite a few shorter plays. I send them nowhere because it is a waste of time, with the situation what it is in the theatre— Broadway is in the real estate and high finance business, off-Broadway is a lot of cliques, the university theatres are kids who can't do anything with half the skill required, and so I let the new plays accumulate.

The Armenian plays were part of Saroyan's perpetual investigation of self and of the fate of modern man; they were especially important in his constant preoccupation with identity. The role Armenians play in William Saroyan's writing has been reexamined recently by David Calonne in *William Saroyan: My Real Work Is Being* (1983), and more insistently argued by James Tashjian in the introduction to *My Name Is Saroyan* (1983). The recent biographies by his son Aram, *William Saroyan* (1983), and by Larry Lee and Barry Gifford, *Saroyan* (1984), with their preoccupation with Saroyan the man rather than the writer, also offer in passing some "Armenian" insights. Rather than repeat information accessible to ardent followers of Saroyan, I prefer to supplement what is already available with unpublished testimony dating from the seventies, when these plays were written, in order to establish a personal context for them.

Saroyan frequently and happily emphasized the importance of his early Fresno years—1916 to 1926. He had returned to his birthplace with his mother, sisters, and brother after five years in the Fred Finch Orphanage in Oakland, California. A decade later, at eighteen, he abandoned Fresno for San Francisco. Nevertheless, the experience remained vital to him. On March 4, 1974, he wrote in his journal:

> During those ten solid years of living in Fresno I made my life, I forged my soul...I recognised and accepted my character, and I made my decision about the kind of life I was going to live, or at any rate try to live. And therefore these ten years were surely as important as any other ten years of my life, and possibly the most important.... And what was the essential of the years in Fresno: they were the years of Armenia, pure and simple: and I mean that they were the years of the Saroyan tribe of the people of the highland city of Bitlis near Lake Van and Mount Ararat, who wrenched themselves loose from their roots going back centuries and traveled by mule and horse and ship and train to California, and down to Fresno. They were most of all the years of self—of this particular member of the Saroyan tribe, this last born of Armenak and Takoohi.

Except for William, the "Californian," the Saroyan children were born in historical Armenia, Cozette and Zabel in Bitlis, Henry in Erzeroum. Both his parents were from Bitlis, both from the Saroyan clan. In Armenian Fresno, the surroundings were old-country family and friends. *My Name Is Aram* is the famous retelling of that world. But we are still uncertain just when Saroyan started using the theater to talk about Armenians. The dates and contents of too many works with suggestive titles remain unknown: plays such as "The Armenian Play (or Opera)," "The Saroyans," or the intriguing "Ouzenk, Chouzenk, Hai Yenk" (literally "Whether We Like It or Not, We Are Armenian"), a play to be performed in Armenian, and according to his friend, artist Varaz Samuelian, one written in an Armenian phonetically spelled with English letters. For the moment, these and others remain provocative items in inventory lists of unpublished Saroyan.

The earliest of the plays that I know of, predominately about or peopled with Armenians, is "Is There Going to Be a Wedding?" written in the first half of 1970. Saroyan presented me with a copy in December 1980, inscribed as "one more Armenian, Fresno, Saroyan play—to read, enjoy, study, and some day produce and perform. . . ." Its forty-one scenes depict the future writer in conflict with family from his pre-teens to age fourteen, but in anticipation of his flight, four years hence. Besides "Willie," the main characters are his brother, Henry; Uncles Aram, the materialistic and pragmatic lawyer, and Mihran, the idealistic and intellectual tailor; Mother Takoohi; other family members and a couple of Armenian priests. In vivid language spiced with American vulgarisms, the play exposes the opposing forces contesting for Saroyan's young soul. But in it the playwright is more interested in the personalities of relatives with whom he interacted as an adolescent than in the purely Amenian dimension of the environment.

In the following year, 1971, an engaged Saroyan pursued his inner quest in *Armenians*, the first play of the trilogy, by combining remembrances of youth and heated discussions about the biting sorrow of loss associated with the national tragedy of his people, with the remarkable continuity of communal life played out before a backdrop of hopelessness. Soon other plays were to follow, each usually treating a single facet of the Armenian predicament. In 1975, during the March and April leading up to the 60th commemoration of the Armenian Genocide, Saroyan was preoccupied with general world indifference to the plight of his people. On March 3 he made a personal note to write "All about the Armenians, a book." During these two months he created no fewer than six works about Armenians for the theater: "Turks in the World," "The Istanbul Comedy," "The Jew" (about Saroyan's incognito visit to a Paris synogogue), *Bitlis*, "Home to Hayastan," and "Mihr." Of these *Bitlis* is the most serious, a personal psycho-drama, a coming to terms with one of the badges of Saroyan's self-definition.

Saroyan wrote *Haratch*, the longest of these Armenian plays, and the most elevated in style and provocative in ideas, less than two years before his death. It was the last major statement he made on his own ethnicity, though it was not the last play in which Armenians were to figure. Exactly a year later, in July, 1980, at the request of Vienna's

English Theatre, Saroyan composed "Tales of the Vienna Streets" a whimsical but serious comedy which takes place in a cafe in the Austrian capital. Thomas Quinn Curtiss, in a pre-view of the play (*International Herald Tribune*, July 31, 1981), describes the cafe owner thus: "Its [the cafe's] generous, inquisitive proprietor is a displaced Armenian who, like Saroyan himself, often utters rousing tributes to his beloved homeland, the greatest of his people and their literature." In what may have been Saroyan's last play, the conversation and ideas are broadly universal, the major characters, archetypes of humanity. The play deserves quick publication, but it does not focus directly, or at least solely, on the Armenian dilemma and, therefore, is not included in this volume.

Armenians, Bitlis, and *Haratch* fit comfortably together for reasons other than the common ethnic origin of their characters. The setting of each is exile. *Armenians*, takes place in 1921 just after the national tragedy when the possibility of return to Armenia seemed a matter of time. Four decades later, the exiled Saroyan actually travels to Bitlis in the play *Bitlis*, and confronts the impossibility of return. In *Haratch*, the problem of exile is posed differently: How is one to adjust to its permanence? However, a central theme in all the plays is something worse than exile, something that Saroyan addressed directly only at the end of his life—genocide. Genocide, the willful murder of a nation, a word invented since World War II, is what Armenians suffered in 1915. It created the diaspora, emptying Armenia of its indigenous population and scattering everywhere those who survived. It is the unspoken calamity underlying these works. How curious that Saroyan, willing and able to render into story or play any subject, was unable to write directly about the Armenian Genocide, about the mass murder and deportations ordered by the Young Turks or even the massacres carried out earlier under Sultan Abdul Hamid in 1894-6 and in 1909. It was precisely to escape future massacres that Saroyan's own family fled to America.

The first plays talk about the Genocide, yet never uttering its name. Even the word *massacre* is missing. In *Armenians* we read, "They all died. They were all killed. . . .I lost them all." But how? In *Bitlis* we are only told that ". . .all of Bitlis was made bereft of its real inhabitants, the Armenians." Again we ask, how? In the same play Saroyan himself says, "I really don't know what happened in the first place, a thousand times in the first place.'' These polite euphemisms are the closest allusions to the event.

Only in *Haratch*—written four years after *Bitlis*, years during which Armenian violence against the symbols of the Turkish state compelled remembrance of what had happened in 1915—did Saroyan boldly state the facts of genocide he knew so well. A few lines from the play are enough to show the change in language. ''How have we had our revenge for the two million Armenians killed by the Turks?'' (Zohrab, p.142). ''We refuse to forget the crime of genocide inflicted upon us by Turkey,'' (Saroyan, p.159).

Whether directly invoked in the last play or indirectly understood in the earlier ones, the Genocide is the genesis of the two major themes in the trilogy: exile, and the survival of a dispersed nation denied the right of repatriation.

The plays follow chronologically. They reveal, through Saroyan's uncanny ability to recreate voices from the past, how the Genocide was perceived at its inception, during his own youth in Fresno thousands of miles away from Armenia; half a century later in Bitlis, Turkish-occupied Armenia; and today, when diverse Armenians from around the world meet by chance in Paris. A perpetual dialogue that begins in *Armenians* among uneducated farmers, unsophisticated clergy, and professional men and continues, unended, in *Haratch* with first-and-second generation professors, poets, and journalists. In 1921, those in the diaspora wonder about the fate of their brothers surviving under desperate conditions in the tiny remnant of Armenia that had arisen from the ashes of genocide in 1918 as a ''free and independent'' Republic. Two years later, it was metamorphosized by force into a Bolshevik Republic, an aftereffect of the Russian Revolution. In 1979 in *Haratch* a second-generation intellectual from that same Soviet Armenian Republic sits in the offices of an Armenian newspaper in the West and discusses with his diasporic counterparts the continuing effects of the Genocide and the question of return. Between them—the Diaspora and the Soviet Republic—lies geographic Armenia empty of Armenians. Around them is a world that, if no longer ignorant of the forgotten Genocide, is certainly indifferent to it.

Bitlis is the link between the desperation of the post-Genocide period and the present, between the hopeful idealism of a time of hopelessness and the energetic realism of today. It is the test of an agonizing quest for a postulated return pitted against the confusion of a real one.

Saroyan, the individual Armenian, lives out the search for the mythic Bitlis, the place that in his mind defined much of his character. Its prevelance is connected to Saroyan's personal identification with its customs, geography, and special dialect. For him, Bitlis is Armenia.

In William Saroyan's final will article three says in part: "I direct that my ashes be delivered to the trustees of the WILLIAM SAROYAN FOUNDATION and that, if possible, one-half (1/2) of my ashes be delivered by the trustees to an appropriate location in Armenia, as determined in the absolute discretion of the trustees." In personal conversations and in earlier versions of the will, Saroyan asked that one-half of his ashes be scattered or deposited in Bitlis once Bitlis again becomes Armenian. He wanted his heart in the Armenian highlands. A year after his death, half of his cremated remains were permanently dignified at the pantheon of greats in Erevan, the capital of Armenia.

Every play of this constructed trilogy, while dealing with the general theme of forced national exile, has its own particular environment, its own context in Saroyan's life. The circumstances of composition and the background of each, as separate preludes to the plays, will be presented below.

ARMENIANS

The earliest of the plays and the only one of the three to have been produced was written in Fresno in twenty-one days, from November 10 to November 30, 1971. In the following year, Archbishop Torkom Manoogian, Primate of the Armenian Diocese of North America, asked Saroyan for an original play on the Armenians that could be produced in the diocesan cathedral in New York City. In 1974 Saroyan sent *Armenians* for its premier presentation.

The production was assigned to Ed Setrakian, an actor and director who had staged *The Time of Your Life* for the Diocese in 1964. By special arrangement with Actor's Equity he put together a cast of professionals for six performances in the Kavookjian Auditorium on October 22, 23, 24, 29, 30, 31, 1974. The audiences were enthusiastic, and New York critics praised the play, its director, and the actors; as a result it was presented four more times in November. In the *Village*

Voice, Arthur Sainer said, "Exciting theatre. . . . Under. . . Setrakian's direction, *Armenians* is alive. . . . The air is filled with exhortations of such dimension that no adequate response seems available." In the *New York Daily News*, Patricia O'Haire wrote, the characters "are so beautifully drawn, so honest and so lifelike that they are universal."

Saroyan did not see the actual production. According to Ed Setrakian, he passed through New York during its preparation, arranged to meet with the cast, and in his usual egregious way, acted out each of the parts. Setrakian adds that Saroyan sent a two-page description identifying each character, but this document has since been lost. Nevertheless, in the letter of March 7, 1975, to his agent, already cited above, Saroyan comments: "This one was done at the cathedral for a limited run, and judging from tapes I asked to have, the thing was done real stupidly, and yet in spite of that the audience and the critics liked it. So there we are. . . . " After listening to the tape recording on November 30, 1974, he wrote the following on his copy of the script now in the Bancroft Library: "Sat. 1230-2 PM. Listened to the tape—stupid and all wrong, good God." Five years later, on Christmas Eve, 1980, in Fresno, he discussed the staging with me more specifically: "Setrakian's production of *The Armenians* was off base. He had them get too shrill, a bogus trick. Armenians are not shrill. [Elia] Kazan also has everybody jumping up and down; tricks, [he] uses lots of tricks." Saroyan's plays, despite their apparent simplicity, are extremely difficult to mount successfully. It was never easy to satisfy him either.

Saroyan referred to *Armenians* (also called *The Armenians*) as a play in twenty-one scenes, even though the uninterrupted action takes place in only two settings. The Setrakian production was, wisely and with the author's blessing, divided into two acts; I have followed that division. The twenty-one scenes of *Armenians*, the seven of *Bitlis*, and the thirty of *Haratch*—exactly equal to the number of pages in each of the original typescripts—originated from the process used by Saroyan to write these and all later plays. There is evidence that his earlier plays may have been written in the same way. Each was composed a page a day on as many consecutive days as needed; Saroyan's single spaced, marginless pages contain 700 to 800 words. The ritual was unvarying; Saroyan never skipped a day, and never spent more than twenty to thirty minutes on a page. He composed at the typewriter without benefit of drafts, outlines, or notes. The intensity of his creation was aided only by reflection in the course of routine activities during the twenty-four hours between sessions. The first draft was always the final one, and none was rewritten.

The action in the original scenes one through seven (Act One) takes place in the Holy Trinity Armenian Apostolic Church in Fresno, still on the corner of Ventura and M Street in the heart of what was once the "Armenian town" of Saroyan's youth. He called it the "Red Brick Church" because of the building material used to erect it in 1914. Act Two, scenes eight through twenty-one, takes place just across Ventura in the Armenian Patriotic Club, called until recent years the Asbarez Club after the Armenian newspaper of that name moved to Los Angeles in 1974. Already twenty years earlier, in the novel *Rock Wagram* (1951), Saroyan has the movie actor-hero pay a sentimental visit to "*The Asbarez* building" in search of the natural warmth of his childhood. The modest landmark was torn down in the early 1980s to make way for a new Holiday Inn, which now faces Holy Trinity on one side and, across M Street, the rebaptized William Saroyan Theatre on the other.

The dramatis personae are in two groups, a genteel middle-class represented by three clergymen and a doctor trained at Harvard, and a collection of men from major cities of historic Armenia: Bitlis, Moush, Van, Kharpert/Harpoot, Erzeroum, Dikranagert/Diyarbekir. Two of the clerics, Father Kasparian, of the Red Brick Church, and Reverend Knadjian, of the First Armenian Presbyterian Church, already appear in secondary roles in Saroyan's "Is There Going to Be a Wedding?" They, like Reverend Papazian, Minister by inference of the Pilgrim Armenian Congregational Church, are based on historical figures. Saroyan wrote from memory of those he had observed; like ancient Greek and Armenian historians, he created imagined dialogue faithful to each. Vardan *vardapet* Kasparian came to Fresno in 1912 from Bursa Turkey, to take charge of Holy Trinity. He remained its spiritual leader for more than twenty years; eventually he attained the rank of archbishop and the post of Primate of the Armenian Church of California. He officiated at the consecration of the "Red Brick Church" in 1914. M. J. Knadjian was Reverend of the First Armenian Presbyterian Church, Saroyan's church, from 1912 to 1922; the original structure on Fulton Street at Santa Clara was built in 1901 and used until 1941. Saroyan describes how he nearly bought the building, still standing today, in a chapter devoted to it and Rev. Knadjian in *Places*

Where I've Done Time (1972). Manaseh G. Papazian (1865-1943) was born in Beredjik, Cilician Armenia. After studying at Yale Divinity and Andover, he returned to Ottoman Turkey with his new American wife to serve in the neighboring city of Aintab. From 1914 to 1940 he was pastor of Pilgrim Armenian Congregational Church. The first building on Van Ness and Inyo Streets was used from 1910 to 1921. Not only in *Armenians*, but in all three plays the characters are consistently modeled on actual people.

In *Armenians*, the mixture of guarded respect and cavalier scepticism toward the clergy is consistent with Saroyan's own attitude toward the church, the only strong Armenian institution in the early diaspora. The first settlers, those who came before World War I, were closely linked to Protestant American missionary activity in Eastern Anatolia. Later refugees were more often tied to the mother church. Then as now Armenian Protestants were more willing to accept Americanization, while Apostolics struggled to preserve language and national sentiment. Saroyan was officially a Protestant; his father had been a sometimes minister of the Presbyterian Church. Though later wary of organized religion, young Saroyan attended church. "Sundays in Fresno were both pleasant and boring for me. Most of the time I hated going to The First Armenian Presbyterian Sunday School, but I went just the same, because it was the rule of the family. I didn't mind too much, because it was possible to have fun there too. Everything was in English, of course, except the major part of Reverend Knadjian's sermon, but we didn't stay for that very often," ("Sunday Is a Hell of a Day," p.18).

On special occasions—mainly funerals and weddings—he also attended the Apostolic "red brick church," which was, like First Presbyterian, near to his house. Close proximity and identification are responsible for the authentic portraits of the clergy in *Armenians* and *Haratch*.

Armenians was motivated by an inner archaeology, a search through memory to recall and then resuscitate forgotten personalities. The catalyst for writing it was the approach of November 29. Until recently the date has been a source of antagonism in the diaspora between fervent supporters of the nationalist Armenian Republic, for whom it represents the disastrous loss of independence, and those who unconditionally defend the Armenian Soviet Socialist Republic, for whom it is the national holiday, the beginning of Soviet Armenia. Saroyan always had difficulty with state authority, and though he loved his visits to Soviet Armenia and was loved and worshipped there, he never gracefully accepted Russian tutelage, as is clear in the play.

The action of *Armenians* takes place neither in 1922, as indicated in the original manuscript, nor in 1920, as Saroyan stated in his Program Note of October, 1974. Consistency with the historical events described demands the year 1921, since in the play the "seat of the government" has fallen to the Russians for the second time. The "free and independent" Republic lasted from May 28, 1918, to November 29, 1920. The government of the majority Dashnak Party, under extreme duress, turned over power to the Communists in exchange for a guarantee of protection from the Nationalist Turkish army that had already invaded and was determined to complete the annihilation started in 1915. So the first seizure of Armenia by the Bolsheviks was in late 1920. Three months later, in February, a general uprising, provoked by dissatisfaction with the new leaders, drove the Communists out of Erevan. But in early April, 1921, the Bolsheviks reentered the capital; by July the revolt was crushed throughout the country and the "Russians"—in reality Armenian Communists supported by the Red Army—were back in the "chair of government" for the second time.

The question troubling those in the Patriotic Club is how to help their brothers thousand of miles away in Armenia. Interwoven with it is another, more elusive, but more immediate problem announced near the beginning of the play: How is one to preserve the Armenian nation, its language and customs, here in America? Despite the humor that saturates the play, these problems were as serious and unresolved then as they are today. Is it better to demonstrate the defiant national spirit by striving to become totally, one hundred percent, American, or by obstinately to remain as Armenian as possible? In 1921 the idea of return was concrete to the adult generation, but for the youth the force of public school, English, and new and "progressive" American ways were all-consuming.

The either/or dilemma of ethnic identity was more painful in Fresno than elsewhere from the 1920s to the 1940s. No other city in the United States has been more closely associated with the Armenians. At the time of the play, they numbered about 15,000 there, the largest concentration in America. Today, the more than 40,000 Armenians in the San Joaquin Valley represent some eight percent of the area's population, still by proportion the highest density in the U.S. A recent centennial exhibit and film documentary, *Strangers in a Promised Land*, on the first Armenian settlement in Fresno (1881-1981) showed a people's achievement in an environmemt of vicious discrimination. No Armenian escaped the bigotry; reaction to it varied, but many took the easier path of assimilation to avoid the added injury of racism after the devastations of genocide.

Saroyan characteristically chose the hard path. Though he was successfully "integrated" into American life, he never suffered the loss of ethnic identity so often coupled with "assimilation." He has written about growing up Armenian in Fresno many times, usually with humor, often with aggressive disdain toward the establishment. Pertinent to and contemporary with these plays is a little-known radio interview Saroyan accorded to Charles Amirkhanian for the Pacifica stations, KPFA in Berkeley and KFCF in Fresno, and broadcast on February 17, 1976. In an hour-long monologue he reminisced about "Growing Up in Fresno," the title of the program. In the following passage Saroyan directly discusses the problem of ethnic attitudes:

> The question comes up: didn't Fresno have a tremendous limit of spirit and mind, and a certain kind of obvious and foolish and mistaken sense of superiority, based upon wealth and class and so on? Well, of course it did, but that is human, and that is everywhere. Well, weren't the Armenian people in Fresno belittled and considered inferior? Yes, they were, by some people, but not by everybody. Well, wasn't it actually universally established in the mind, if you could call it that, of the town and the region, that the Armenian was something else, as the saying is? Yes, that was true, too. Well, what effect did that have on me? Well, it had little effect. I think it had a good effect. It certainly made it necessary for me to acknowledge to myself first that I am who I am—an Armenian—and not somebody who does not wish to be an Armenian, but somebody who accepts that he is an Armenian in an atmosphere where the Armenian is disliked; at the very least, we can put it that way. And that I must make known to anybody who dislikes Armenians that I am one of them. I am an Armenian.

In *Armenians*, the ethnic debate is conducted by juxtaposition of characters rather than by sustained arguments (these would be

developed later in *Haratch*). Various problems are posed, but few are
settled. This was Saroyan's way: by formulating a question clearly
the reader was compelled to understand its dimensions, after which
he was nudged toward, if not its solution, at least its resolution.
However, some problems persisted, often because the questions of
Saroyan's youth remained the same when he wrote the
play: unanswered and, until now, unanswerable. "Why does God give
the Armenian so little to thank him for?" Why should surviving victims
of genocide feel guilty because they survived when nearly everybody
else did not? The voice of the people, common farmer and laborer,
is more eloquently heard in this play than the others: "We can stop
mourning, but we cannot forget." The orderly politeness of middle
class, Anglo-Saxon comportment is directly challenged by the
powerful: "The people...refuse to be polite about indestructible
Armenia."

In *Armenians* Saroyan saw the life of the expatriate as discouraging,
but one impelled by dignified though endless struggle. Speaking for
the nation, his own summation in the Program Note is typically a
paradox, a verbal sleight-of-hand. "The play *Armenians* perhaps says,
It's hopeless and we know it, but not so hopeless that we don't want
to find out how hopeless it is."

BITLIS

Bitlis is the story of a voyage, a passage to the town of the same
name that Saroyan made in 1964. Of the plays in the trilogy, it is the
most personal. It was written on seven successive mornings starting
Sunday, March 23, and ending Saturday, March 29, 1975, an average
of twenty-eight minutes spent on each of its seven pages and a total
compositional time of three and one-half hours. He had publicly
declared eleven years earlier that he would write a play describing
his trip; he had, after all, prepared a lifetime to go to Bitlis. Why did
Bitlis need eleven years of gestation before it could be spat out whole
in less than four hours? What conjunction of events in March 1975
provoked or inspired Saroyan to do it then?

Two answers are easily suggested. Other, less tangible ones become
apparent only when Saroyan's earlier associations with the city of Bitlis
are made clear and his preoccupations of the moment are examined.
Let us begin with the easy answers.

First, 1975 was particularly creative for Saroyan, especially for theatrical works which were written with journalistic rapidity. During three months, thirteen weeks from Sunday, February 16 to Saturday, May 17, Saroyan wrote plays every single morning, producing at least seventeen. Writing had become an obsession. Each was in one act, each was seven pages long (his seven scenes), and each was begun on a Sunday morning. *Bitlis* was the ninth. The eighth, "The Human Head," a spoof on psychoanalysis, was written on the same mornings, but a half hour earlier.

Sixteen of these plays remain in manuscript. *Bitlis* was first published in the special Saroyan issue of the quarterly *Ararat* (Spring 1984) by permission of the estate of William Saroyan. It was among the "Armenian plays," as he called them. There are only two settings: the action of the first six pages of the typescript takes place in a restaurant, while the last moments of the play unfold in a Chevrolet, as Saroyan and his friends drive away from Bitlis toward other cities of historic Armenia.

A second reply to why the play was written when it was is also apparent. If four years earlier the approach of November 29 had been motivation enough to write *Armenians*, in the spring of 1975, the approach of April 24, the day the Genocide began sixty years before, was an occasion for writing *Bitlis*. Saroyan had a fetish about dates; his birthday, August 31, was the most important in his personal calendar. Projects were started or finished on chosen days, such as the unpublished autobiographical "Fifty-Fifty," begun the day after his fiftieth birthday and finished a year later on August 31, 1959. *Bitlis* became part of his contemplation of April 24th, 1975.

Once again, to write this play Saroyan engaged in psychic archaeology in order to penetrate the world of recollections. In March, 1975, he struggled to remember and make sense of his visit to Bitlis— a confusing experience from the recent past.

Though Saroyan was born in Fresno, when with close friends he always said, he was from Bitlis. That is, in the Armenian fashion, he proclaimed himself a "Bitlistsi," using the suffix -tsi/-etsi which renders "of" or "from" when added to a place name. The attachment was strong, a source of pride. The ancestoral hometown of his parents and grandparents as far back as memory was his, too.

In Armenia, regional pride was as strong as in any country. Bitlis had its own Armenian dialect, which William Saroyan spoke (though

William Saroyan's interest in Armenian life began during his childhood in Fresno. On several occasions he wrote about General Antranik, modern Armenia's greatest military hero, whose impressive funeral procession in Fresno, where he died on August 30, 1927, made a permanent mark on Saroyan. He used to visit Antranik's grave and monument in Paris at the Père-Lachaise Cemetery, where he is shown (above) in May 1974. (Photo Ed Hagopian) Below, Saroyan bows his head before the general's monument in Erevan, Armenia. (Photo SPIURK: Committee for Cultural Relations with Armenians Abroad)

In 1976 on the third of his four visits to Armenia, Saroyan is greeted at Erevan airport with the traditional Armenian flat bread and salt, a sign of welcome and hospitality. Just behind him are poet Razmik Davoyan and Vartkes Petrossian, President of the Armenian Writers Union. Below, Saroyan kneels before the eternal flame of the memorial in Erevan to the 1,500,000 victims of the Genocide of 1915. (Photos SPIURK)

Saroyan planting a tree in Armenia. The elderly gentlemen in the background is Vartkes Hamazaspian, Director of the Committee for Cultural Relations with Armenians Abroad or SPIURK as it is called in Armenian. (Photo P. H. Boghosian, SPIURK)

In 1976 Saroyan visited Geghart, the famous medieval Armenian monastery carved out of solid rock. Above, he is seen with a priest of the monastery. The white-haired gentleman to the left is Saroyan's dear friend and fellow Bitlistsi, Aram-Ashot Babayan, one of Armenia's best loved playwrights. Below, Saroyan is received at Etchmiadzin, Armenia by another good friend, His Holiness Vasken I, Catholicos of All Armenians, who performed a special requiem mass for Saroyan in Paris on the first Sunday, May 24, 1981, after the author's death. (Photos SPIURK)

Accompanying Saroyan to Armenia in 1976 was his friend from Fresno, the sculptor Varaz Samuelian, who was born in Erevan. He is seen above to the right, just behind Saroyan, during an interview in Erevan. Below, Saroyan is surrounded by a group of Armenian intellectuals in Erevan, 1976: from left to right, Vartkes Hamazaspian, Vartkes Petrossian, who came to Fresno in the summer of 1981 for the Saroyan Tribute at the Convention Center, and Victor Hampartzumian, President of the Armenian Academy of Sciences and world famous astro-physicist. (Photos SPIURK)

William Saroyan [signature]

IS THERE GOING TO BE A WEDDING?

A Play

by

William Saroyan

For Dickran Kouymjian and his Armenian Studies at the University — one more Armenian, Fresno, Saroyan play — to read, enjoy, study, & some day produce & perform — good luck

William Saroyan [signature]

2729 West Griffith Way
Fresno, California 93705

Sat Dec 13 1980

Though in his writings Saroyan seldom alluded to his unpublished plays about the Armenians, he thought of them as forming a group as the inscribed title page of ''Is There Going to Be a Wedding?''—a ribald autobiographical play of 1970 set in Fresno during his early teens—shows. (Courtesy of Dickran Kouymjian)

In the last six months of his life Saroyan had drawn up a series of three new wills leaving his literary estate to the William Saroyan Foundation, established by him years earlier. On October 21, 1980 he asked Professor Dickran Kouymjian to invite a group of California State University, Fresno dignitaries to witness the signing of the first of these wills, which, like the others to follow, recognized CSU, Fresno as one of the repositories for his archives. Center, Saroyan with the late Leon Peters, the second witness of the will of October 21, 1980, after the ceremony. On April 11, 1981, Saroyan signed a third and final will, this one drawn up by lawyers Robert Damir of San Francisco and Aram Kevorkian of Paris, who is shown below with Saroyan at the signing. Saroyan died the following month, May 18, 1981.

(Top and center photos, Dickran Kouymjian; bottom photo taken by Penny Console for the Cal. State Univ., Fresno Armenian Studies Program)

According to Saroyan's will one-half of his ashes were to be taken to Armenia. In May 1982 the William Saroyan Foundation sent half the ashes to Erevan in a polished bronze urn with a delegation headed by Foundation lawyer Robert Damir. The urn (above) had been inscribed by Leon Peters as follows: "William Saroyan. Author and Humanitarian. Born in Fresno, California 1908-1981." In Erevan Saroyan's friend Aram-Ashot Babayan had the other side similarly inscribed in Armenian. On Saturday, May 29, 1982, William Saroyan's ashes were carried to the gravesite in the "Komitas Pantheon" on a bier. Below, the Premier and First Secretary of the Communist Party of the Armenian Soviet Socialist Republic, Garen Demirjian, is seen as one of the pallbearers. Below, at four o'clock in the afternoon, following three hours of speeches and ceremonies, the urn was placed in a grave and covered over with a concrete slab and earth. (Photos Dickran Kouymjian)

he never learned to read Armenian). Its inhabitants were famous for distinctive character traits: pride, scorn, and toughness. To write about Bitlis was a serious affair, one that evoked a past full of the wild escapades of crazy relatives, but also a past haunted with melancholy, pain, and loss. More than anything else, Bitlis was the place of Armenak, his father who died when Saroyan was three, and who, at thirty-six, was an unfulfilled farmer, minister, and poet. His longing to see and to find Bitlis was inseparable from a lifelong search for his father.

Though he had never seen Bitlis, it was vivid in his mind through the precise and repeated descriptions of his mother, uncles, and especially maternal grandmother, Lucintak. He had read and owned the pitiful account of Grace H. Knapp, *The Tragedy of Bitlis*, published in 1919 shortly after the massacres. He had himself written about the mountain city just west of Lake Van, its river, its hills, and its adjacent villages, more than once. In the 1942 story, "The Man Who Knew My Father as a Boy in Bitlis," these themes are tied together. Places mentioned in it, like the nearby village of Gultik and the fountain at Tsapergor, are in later works. "Hayastan and Charentz," written in 1954, begins: "Two things sent me to Hayastan (i.e. Armenia) in the spring of 1935 when I was twenty-six years old: a writer's restlessness, and a son's need to see his father's birthplace." A little further he continues: "I was not unaware that in reaching Soviet Armenia I would not be reaching my father's Armenia, or his city, Bitlis. It was enough at that time to reach the general vicinity of my father's birthplace, and to be in a nation named Armenia, inhabited by Armenians." Is not the phrase "enough at that time" a clear indication, as early as 1954, of a future pilgrimage to Bitlis?

Another story about his father, "Armenak of Bitlis" (1968), remarkably has nothing concrete about Bitlis in it. What had happened in between the detailed descriptions of the 1954 story and the failure to describe in 1968? In the spring of 1964 Saroyan went to Bitlis. He confessed however, he was unable to put it in writing until later. Some months after the trip, on September 22, 1964 he wrote to his traveling companion Bedros Zobian: "It was a grand tour, one of the most important pieces of travel and exploration I have ever made, but very very difficult for me to write about. . . . And so, I have no immediate plans to even try to write about it." In *Haratch*, he says as one of his own characters, "I did get to Bitlis a good thirteen or fourteen years ago. . .When I got back to Fresno I didn't know where to start, and in the end the only thing I wrote was a kind of poem called Bitlis, but it does not really tell what is in my heart to tell, which I don't really know how to tell." Had Saroyan's usually sharp memory faltered? Or was the experience so unsettling he repressed it? Why did he fail to mention the play *Bitlis* instead of referring to "a kind of poem?" The poem "Bitlis" and a fifty-two page manuscript of the same name written in 1969—neither of which I have seen—are registered among his unpublished works. The latter, which begins "Bitlis is a city," and ends "I was glad to be leaving Bitlis," was probably the work completed in the summer of 1967 in Paris and mentioned in an inscription from one of Saroyan's books: "September 19, 1967. . .during July and August the following works were wrought. . . .6. Bitlis, a kind of free examination of a place, and a visit to it." Saroyan was disoriented by the visit; not only are there no references to it in a work like *Places Where I've Done Time* (1972), but he failed to speak of it in a long interview of May 1975, just two months after the play was written. In a January 21, 1977 letter to Zobian, he says "Why did I not write about our great 1964 tour of Anatolia, of Armenia and our visits to all of our magnificent places? I wrote a kind of poem called Bitlis which I shall have published some day, but I believe I was unable to write a full book because I knew I would become angry about our story and there are already so many of us who have written out of such anger." Had he actually forgotten or repressed the writing of the play until the last year of his life? Perhaps some day, in addition to the insights into *Bitlis* itself, his journals will help explain this phenomenon better.

Apart from his feverish writing mood and the arrival of the sixtieth commemoration of the Genocide, what else compelled him to write *Bitlis* in March 1975? I have pointed out elsewhere that Saroyan was struck by Michael Arlen's *Passage to Ararat*, originally a three-part *New Yorker* "Profile" in February of that same year. The dimensions of Arlen's literary as well as his actual voyage to Armenia in search of his father and inherited ethnicity often echoed Saroyan's own emotional saga. In this suggestive and penetrating book, and the personal search it describes, Saroyan played an important role; at moments he even served as surrogate father. An entire section is devoted to Arlen's visit with him in Fresno, and it was the senior writer who told him to go to Armenia. The reading of *Passage to Ararat*, simultaneously a quest for the real and the symbolic Armenia, inspired Saroyan to describe his own search, his own passage. On October 24, 1975, after Saroyan returned to Fresno, he wrote the following to James Tashjian, editor of *The Armenian Review*: "What he [Arlen] has done in *Passage to Ararat* could not have been done by anybody else in the whole world or in all of the dimensions and channels of sequential time—it had to be Dickran Kouyoumdjian's [Arlen senior's real name] puzzled son with a totally different personality, style, talent, and aspiration: we are all of us lucky it happened, for these things need luck," (*The Armenian Review*, September, 1981, p.337).

Saroyan set out for Bitlis in April, 1964. On the first of May he arrived in Istanbul via Israel and Cyprus. Upon his arrival he met Bedros Zobian, co-editor and publisher of the Armenian daily *Marmara*. Saroyan told him of his plans to go to Bitlis. Zobian says he asked how he would go; Saroyan said, by taxi. He reminded Saroyan that it was about a 1000 miles from Istanbul and offered to accompany him. Zobian, his friend Ara Altounian, a business man and industrialist, and Saroyan left the capital for Bitlis by car on May 9, 1964. They returned to Istanbul sixteen days later on the 25th. Zobian's detailed reportage for *Marmara* began to appear even before their return. Because of Saroyan's popularity—some have said he is the most famous Armenian of all time—the articles were reprinted or mentioned in Armenian papers throughout the diaspora. In contrast to Saroyan's literary version of the trip, below is a circumstantial summary of Zobian's chronicle based on articles appearing in *Haratch* of Paris on May 20, 22, 27, 28, 29, 1964, and a recent detailed letter from him.

The trio drove straight to Ankara, then north to the Black Sea coastal cities of Samsun, Giresun, and Trebizond, places with important Armenian communities before the deportations of 1915. Moving south toward the interior of eastern Anatolia (historic Armenia), they went to Erzeroum and Van, the city and lake, spending the afternoon admiring the famous tenth century Armenian church on the nearby island of Aghtamar. Saroyan was doubly pleased, because in Van he was told an official reception would be waiting for him at Bitlis. From Tatvan on the opposite side of the lake, where they were lodged, they headed toward Bitlis. The closer they got, the more nervous and excited Saroyan became. According to Zobian, Saroyan said, "Nothing can stop me from entering Bitlis tomorrow" (that is, Sunday May 17). As they approached, Saroyan insisted on driving the car into Bitlis.

He excused himself for perspiring so much; he remarked on how hard his heart was beating.

On the outskirts of the city, Saroyan was greeted with bouquets of freshly picked wildflowers from the mountains of Bitlis. Once in the city, he said he needed no guide because he knew it all by heart from the many times the city was described in his childhood. He shouted: "Bitlis, Bitlis, Bitlis." As they walked to the district of Tsapergor, he rejoiced in saying, "I know all of this. I know the old trees. I am a Bitlistsi! My father walked on these roads." He met the mayor; he smoked a cigarette made from Bitlis tobacco. An old man guided him to the vestiges of a stone house he insisted belonged to Saroyan's own family. He was photographed before the ruined hearth. "It's a good place to live forever, the people are good, the flowers good. It's an unforgettable day."

Saroyan and his entourage walked around town for two hours, then went up to the massive fort that dominates the city. There a performing bear put his paw on Saroyan's shoulder. He judged that a good omen. The bear danced, while he announced, "I'm going to write a play with the title 'Bitlis.' He hugged various villagers who came to meet him. It was the most wonderful day of his life, he said. They went to the fountain where he drank deeply. "It's good water. See this city, it's a great city."

After the day in Bitlis they returned to Tatvan and the following day left for Moush, Diyarbekir, and Elazig-Kharpert (Harpoot), because so many of his friends in Fresno were originally from that city. In Erzeroum, Saroyan proposed a new play, "The Istanbul Comedy," modeled on his earlier "The London," "The Paris," and "The Moscow" comedies. Fikret Otyam, a well known Turkish journalist from the popular daily *Cumhuriyet*, guaranteed it would premier simultaneously in seven or eight cities in Turkey if Saroyan gave permission. All proceeds, he added, would go toward equipment for Turkish grammar schools. Saroyan said, "I'll go home to Paris, think about my experience for six months, and write the play in six days, so help me God." This "scoop" was first published in *Marmara* on May 24.

Before reaching Istanbul they visited Antakya, Iskenderun, Adana, the medieval Armenian castle of Yilan Kalesi, Mersin, Antalya, Izmir, and Pamukkale. Saroyan remained in Istanbul until June 1, meeting with the Turkish press. The Armenian Patriarch of Constantinople,

Archbishop Shnork Kaloustian, invited him to lunch. It took him some years to live up to his promises, but in the end, in addition to writing the promised *Bitlis*, three weeks earlier in March 1975, he also wrote "The Istanbul Comedy" in seven days. It is an hilarious play, but at the same time a rude condemnation of the discrimination practiced against the Armenian remnant living in modern Turkey; one would be hard pressed to imagine what Turkish theatrical group would have courage enough to produce it with Armenian-Turkish relations as they are today.

William Saroyan went to Bitlis in search of his roots long before Michael Arlen found Ararat or Alex Haley, Africa. He did not find Armenia or Armenians, but exactly what he must have known he would find: Kurds, who strangely resembled certain of his relatives. He saw Bitlis, the river, the fortress; he walked up and down its sharply inclined streets; visited the area that supposedly had been inhabited by the Saroyans, and saw the hearth of what was said to be his father's house. The one ninety year old Armenian still living in the town knew nothing about the Saroyan family; his only wish was to leave for Beirut to die among Armenians. Zobian says Saroyan combined elements from an older Armenian in Moush and an Armenian father and son from the village of Gultik. Saroyan was overwhelmed, thrilled, confused, perplexed.

Which Bitlis is the real one? That of his forefathers? The one in Saroyan's mind? The one of today? The real Bitlis is both the same and different from the *Bitlis* of Saroyan's creative imagination. To sort it all out he needed time; he took eleven years. In the play, some problems are resolved, others suspended, but through it Saroyan consolidated and reestablished his claim on Bitlis, and, therefore, the Armenian claim to the homeland. He did this by willful, existential choice: "I choose to love Bitlis and to believe that it is ours. Of course I choose. I have no choice but to choose. But since I do choose, that is it, is it not, that is the truth of it, I love Bitlis, I believe it is ours, it is mine" (*Bitlis*, p.107).

On May 25, 1975 in Paris, shortly after *Bitlis* was written, Saroyan gave a long interview to the poet Garig Basmadjian subsequently published in the Saroyan issue of *Ararat* (Spring, 1984, pp.36-7). Though the play is not alluded to, Saroyan reflects on Bitlis and about being Armenian.

GB: Is your Armenian background the best element of your literary output?

WS: Yes, yes, in the sense of my being anything. That is: what usage do you make of your identity? What usage do you make of the accident of what you are? . . . .

GB: Were you ever an American?

WS: Always.

GB: You are always an American, and you were always an Armenian. Let's talk a little about this duality.

WS: Definitely. . . . We are a product of two things well-known and established by everybody. The inherited and the environmental. I am an American by environment. I am an Armenian, that's who I am. I was born an Armenian. But you put me in California, that's my home. So somebody told me "What does California mean to you?" I said, to be perfectly honest, it's my native land. I have a very deep attachment to it. He says "As much as to Hayastan?" Yes, as much as to Hayastan, as much as to Bitlis. In an allegorical rather than sentimental sense, Bitlis is supreme. But this is another dimension of experience. This is almost a dream. This is almost beyond anything that we need try to measure in terms of the reasonable, because, remember, Bitlis has become a kind of monument of our loss. And I have a feeling about regaining, which is almost psychopathic. I wrote a book called *Tracy's Tiger* [1951] in which the theme of regaining the lost is mad, insane, obsessive. This son-of-a-bitch tries to bring back the past, and that is madness. But in regard to Bitlis I know it's beyond any further expectation. I was there ten years ago. I didn't want to leave. But it's not ours. It *is* ours but other people occupy it. I did long for the day when it would be ours and I'd go there. I would go there. Go there and live there. I would settle down there and die there, and put the bones with the other Saroyans that have died there for maybe who knows. Forever. Our bones are there. We are there, as far as memory of our old timers goes; *Saroyannere hos en, ouskitz ekan?* [The Saroyans are here, where did they come from?].

"Forever," said Saroyan. An alternate title for the play was precisely "Bitlis Forever or Never." Saroyan was fond of paradox, insisting on it as a way to begin to see problems clearly. In *Bitlis* the problem of loss and return is resolved. Midway through, Bedros says, "Is this the only Bitlis?...When you put up a new house on land of your own is not the land and the house Bitlis?" (p.107). Later, the argument is consolidated. Bedros: "...Our story does not really permit us anything like common simple gladness about our country." This is further rationalized in the final dialogue by Ara: "...We do not need the childish support of a geographical country to enjoy being who we are.... And who really cares or needs to know why an Armenian happens to be sad, going away from Bitlis...an Armenian is sad because of far, far better reasons than geography and arrival and departure....[But it] saddens me... and makes me break into song, so sing with me about eating bread and drinking wine, that's all" (p.112).

There is neither optimism nor pessimism in this ending, just as there is neither at the end of *Armenians*. In the latter, since the problem is not one that Fresno Armenians can solve, they decide to get on with living. In *Bitlis*, since the dilemma is beyond control, the decision is to enjoy rather than grieve.

Saroyan's return to the mythical Bitlis had been accomplished. The old myth was destroyed; a new one was created.

HARATCH

Haratch, the last sustained treatment of an Armenian theme by Saroyan, is at once the longest, densest, and most serious of the three plays. *Haratch*, which, as the play explains, means "forward," is an Armenian daily in Paris founded in 1925 by Schavarch Missakian. Since his death in 1957, Missakian's daughter, Arpik, has been editor and publisher. With offices at 83 Rue d'Hauteville in the tenth arrondissement, the paper has always been located in what used to be the center of Armenian life in the city. Living close by, Saroyan was fond of dropping in at *Haratch*, which, like Samuelian's bookstore on Rue Monsieur-le-Prince in the Latin Quarter, was and is a gathering place for Armenian writers and intellectuals to exchange news and just talk.

In 1958, after six years of living on the Pacific, Saroyan left his Malibu house. Two years later he bought a flat in the ninth arrondissement of Paris not far from the Opera. Three years after that, in 1963, he also restruck roots in Fresno, buying a modest tract house, and later the one next door. Perhaps this resettling in Fresno where, as in Paris, he was once more in an Armenian milieu, inspired Saroyan and drove him to Bitlis the following spring. During the last decades of his life, he alternated between these places with no fixed pattern, though spring and summer were his preferred Paris seasons.

If Saroyan's life in Paris was not totally reclusive, neither was it similar to that of other expatriate American writers. He did not seek the notoriety of a Hemingway or a Gertrude Stein. He never learned much French either. He did write an occasional column for the *International Herald Tribune* and his works were translated into French. Yet he loved Paris and walked its streets endlessly, as much as any American writer had ever done. He savored Parisian life, especially that of its central quarter, developing a fine sense of the habits of the average Frenchman. He would have been pleased by the plaque put on the facade of his 74 Rue Taitbout walkup this year commemorating his long residence in the city.

During the season in Paris, he associated with old friends and relatives passing through. The more permanent friendships were predominantly with Armenians, usually unpretentious ones rather than community notables. He was never much attracted to the affluent or members of the establishment. His life was given over to reflection and writing, interspersed with travel.

In *Rock Wagram*, Saroyan uses a newspaper office to talk about the destiny of Armenians. While in Fresno, during an impetuous visit to the presses of *Asbarez*, the hero, Arak Vagramian (Rock), is reminded that his dead father once worked for the paper. Poetically, the underlying meaning of the paper is explained: "Rock looked at everything in the place, for a man *is* the vagrant parts of many men scattered and left desolate in many places, in rooms and in machinery, at tables and within walls" (p.99). "You have come here to remember your father," says Krikorian, the editor, quickly toasting with raki "the Armenians, whoever they are, and to their language, whose majesty we all know, lost as it may be forever" (p.101). The short scene fuses father and fatherland while invoking the newspaper as the bearer of the word in a language unsung by the youth of its users.

If church hall and coffee house-patriotic club are the proper settings to discuss the problems in *Armenians*, the ideas put forward in *Haratch* command an ambiance at once more elevated and literate, a place for the dissemination, if not the creation, of ideas. At the same time it is a place of relaxed intimacy. ''Armenians are never so at home as when they are in an editorial office,'' we are told near the end of *Haratch* (p.177).

A permutation is evident in Saroyan's choice of characters. Only a token gesture is made to the anonymous masses—the farmers and workers that appear in *Armenians*—through an octogenarian from Bitlis, who is able to intrude only because he is a writer of the experiences of his youth. Mesrob Ter-Krikorian was his real name; now deceased, he was probably the person mentioned by Saroyan in the earlier Basmadjian interview: ''I love that crazy Bitlistsi, you remember him, don't you? What a wonderful man, eighty-seven years old.'' The simple clergy of the first play are abandoned in *Haratch* for Bishop Stepan, modeled on the Archbishop of Paris, Serovpe Manougian, who, for more than twenty years until his death in 1984 was head of the Armenian Church in Europe. Not only was he a close acquaintance, but the Bishop's niece, Abigail Sarkisian, a nurse at the Veteran's Hospital in Fresno, was a dear friend who attended Saroyan during his final illness.

Among the other interlocutors are journalists and writers. Two— Arpik of *Haratch* and, from Soviet Armenia, Hrachia (Hovannissian) of *Sovetakan grakanoutiwn (Soviet Literature)*—are editors, like Bedros Zobian in *Bitlis*. The others are regular contributors to *Haratch*: Zulal (Zoulal) Kazandjian, poet and teacher at the Armenian Mekhitarist College in Sèvres; Anoushavan Kapikian, custom bootmaker by profession and at eighty-seven still a habitue at *Haratch*; and Zohrab Mouradian, a tailor now aged sixty-seven, also a regular at *Haratch*.

Of the remaining characters, two are young Americans: Khachig Tölölyan, the figure who expresses the most militant ideas in the play, a professor of literature at Wesleyan College—born in Aleppo, raised in Beirut, educated in New England—and his Armenian-American companion, Sylvia, a real estate investment analyst—born in Beirut, raised in Washington and Los Angeles—whose real name is Sylvia Siranoosh Missirlian. During Tölölyan's summer visits to Paris he wrote regularly for *Haratch* while using the offices as headquarters; to this day he remains a regular contributor. Finally, there is Saroyan himself—Bitlistsi, Armenian, American, writer, and Parisian.

Every one of the characters is real and keeps his or her name in the play except for the bishop and "the man from Bitlis." The tailor Agamian, with whom Hrachia stayed, was probably Etvart Aghamian, though another close friend of Saroyan's, Krikor Atamian, was also a tailor. Bringing them all together at the same time in the offices of *Haratch* is theatrical and imaginary. However, Saroyan had met most of them there, and saw the others regularly, like Bishop Manougian and Hrachia Hovannissian, neither of whom, according to Madame Missakian, had ever visited the Rue d'Hauteville offices. Whether Saroyan actually discussed the many topics in the play with the characters in it can only be confirmed or denied by them after reading the words he put into each of their mouths.

Haratch was written in Paris on thirty consecutive afternoons from June 23 to July 22, 1979, less than two years before Saroyan's death. During the same thirty days he wrote his essay-memoir *Births*, published posthumously in 1983. A comparison of the two texts shows no resemblance in either subject or style, except for casual references to Armenians in *Births* (surprisingly few compared to the companion volume *Obituaries*). Saroyan worked on the memoir first, starting about noon, then turned to the play, a more serious and cohesive work. The lighter *Births* served as a warm-up for *Haratch*, much like the more humorous "The Human Head" did for *Bitlis* in March 1975. As with *Bitlis* and *Births*, only a few minutes each day were consecrated to *Haratch*, an average twenty-two and one-half to be precise, which we know because as usual the starting and quitting time was typed at the top and bottom of each page. For the curious, the indications are retained in the printed text of *Births*. As are with all the late plays, no acts were designated in the manuscript, just a scene for each page. However, there are natural breaks, one at the start of page ten of the original, when Sylvia asks, "What is it exactly that Armenians want?" Another begins on page twenty-three when Zulal begins a discussion of poetry. These divide the whole into roughly three equal segments, designated in this edition as acts. Act One functions as a general introduction presenting a variety of questions, some of which are intensely debated in Act Two, while the final section, by a gradual decrescendo resolves certain of them and holds others in suspension.

The central action in *Haratch* is talk, dialogue, the liberal exchange of ideas. The subject is being Armenian. What is it to be Armenian today? To be an Armenian living outside Armenia? There are other questions, too, including some of the same found in *Armenians* and *Bitlis*. None is haphazardly considered, as they were occasionally in the other two works. Rather, Saroyan has chosen individuals from diverse components of the nation—diasporan as well as Soviet Armenian writers, old-time survivors and youthful intellectuals, poets, a high-ranking clergyman, European and American Armenians, and the great writer-personality, William Saroyan—all able to articulate complex problems.

Saroyan by Saroyan: this is something notable. In none of his early successes, or in *Armenians*, does Saroyan appear as a character. But in the intimate "Is There Going to Be a Wedding?" and in *Bitlis* and *Haratch* Saroyan takes the stage. In these plays the writer creates a different dynamic, one that attracts deeper interest in the lines he gives himself. Few playwrights have done this. Indeed, a separate study of Saroyan's "Saroyan plays" exploring this technique would be intriguing. The earliest use of the method must be in "An Imaginary Character Named Saroyan," a play I have not seen, but that he talked about on several occasions. His very last theatrical effort, "Warsaw Visitor," written in 1980 less than a year before his death, also features the writer as principal character, as does his shorter play of 1975, "Dreams of Reality."

In *Haratch* Saroyan is certainly the main character, the animator of the dialogue. As I have suggested in another essay, Saroyan functions in it as Socrates did in the dialogues of Plato. What else is *Haratch* than a modern Socratic dialogue? Furthermore, by its amplitude and specific intrinsic elements, I believe it is consciously modeled on Plato's *Symposium*, with "being Armenian" substituted for "love" as its subject. And as wine was used at the banquet that inspired the *Symposium*, so whiskey, the drink of modern writers, serves amidst the printing presses to expand the imagination and loosen the tongue.

Haratch is a play of ideas. A summary of them would fall beyond the capacity of this introduction. Certain universal ones are basic to Saroyan's position on the perennial matters debated by Armenians and other minorities who have suffered forced exile. Much of the argument is again rendered through paradox. Saroyan described the Armenian paradox a few days before starting on *Bitlis* in a tribute of March 18, 1975, for the 50th anniversary volume of *Haratch*. "But what is the Armenian paradox? It is that against all probabilities we have not only survived history, we have flourished.... We have flourished with heartening effectiveness in our fragmented Soviet Armenia, with both the protection and permission of our Russian brothers and friends, and we have flourished equally forcefully and effectively all over the world, without leave of anybody's protection or permission. That is the Armenian paradox" (*Haratch 50*, Paris, 1976, p.384). As we see in this example, Saroyan juxtaposes conflicting and contradictory views, as though by merely stating them they would become reconciled. In a world of questions, paradoxes, and complexity, where one argument sounds as reasonable as another, Saroyan insists that each person's destiny is determined by his or her own decisions.

Saroyan again articulates an existential world view. For him, being is becoming: by consciously choosing at each moment to do or to be one thing or another you determine what you eventually become. Choosing one's environment, which for Saroyan encompasses one's self-definition, predicates who you are much more than heredity, the accident of birth. How else is one to explain the following dialogue in the very middle of the play? Saroyan asks, "Who is an Armenian?" Zulal replies, "An Armenian is a Turk who says I am an Armenian. It is a decision open to all people, and only Armenians have ever wanted to be Armenians, everybody else has not made a decision but has gone right on being whatever it was he believed he was, anyhow. You have got to choose to be an Armenian, you have got to want to be an Armenian" (pp.153-4). Making the choice requires knowledge of the once-glorious past, as well as the anxiety of exile, of foreignness, of being a victim of genocide.

So that no one should imagine he believed there was any special virtue in being or claiming to be Armenian, Saroyan stressed the point in these plays and elsewhere. Dr. Jivelekian, "While I am not prepared to remark that there really is nothing special about being an Armenian, I also cannot say that fact alone permits any of us to believe we are entitled to anything anybody else is not entitlted to" (*Armenians*, p.69). Saroyan put into *Haratch* his famous corollary to the axiom: Hrachia. "I am sure we have all read it in at least two or three books... everybody is an Armenian, is that not so, Saroyan, did you not say so somewhere?" Saroyan. "Oh, yes, I did, but I was informed that a Jewish writer had said the same thing a year or two before I had done so—or was it a month or two. He said and how right he was: Everybody is a Jew. In other words, everybody is everybody else" (p.169). In Saroyan's system we are incapable of escaping each other's destiny; as human beings we share the totality of all experience.

It is precisely this philosophy of choice that allowed Saroyan to escape the paradox that Bitlis was his, yet not his, that it was Armenian, yet not. In *Bitlis* he suggests that, in addition to the geographic entity west of Lake Van, there is a Bitlis of the spirit actualized wherever a man of Bitlis establishes his roots and lives his life. Bitlis is the symbol of Armenia, the loss of the geographical nation, and the recreation of the diasporic one. Indisputably, this is a message of hope for Saroyan, a suggestion that Armenia can exist away from the ancestral lands as long as there exists a community of individuals consciously choosing it to be.

The theme of a resurrected Armenia is already present in *Armenians*: Man from Moush, "We are Armenians, and even though we are eight thousand miles away from where we were born, we are still in Armenia, we are still there, and this very place, this patriotic coffee house, is Armenia" (p.80). In *Haratch*, the native of Soviet Armenia on a visit to the diaspora says of the newspaper office: ". . .I am home, I am in Armenia in this place" (p.162). During the moment of the play, *Haratch* is Armenia; wherever Armenians come together they reestablish Armenia. The very coming together, by choice, in exile, is the redeeming experience of the nation. The struggle to remain Armenian is its own noble reward.

The diaspora may be anarchic and divisive, but it is a law onto itself. It allows a national existence without land, without war; in Michael Arlen's words, it allows "the capacity of a people for proceeding *beyond* nationhood," without inheriting "territory, and pride in property, or to be connected to collective dreams of quite impossible grandeur and savagery, fertility and hatred" (*Passage to Ararat*, pp.291-2). Whether there is agreement or not, unity or disunity, hope or futility, the important thing is the collective celebration of identity, the assembly and discussion, the Socratic arrival at truth through dialogue. "Who shall remember us if we don't? Who shall remember the Armenians if they don't remember themselves?" Saroyan asks near the end of the play (p.179). Constant choice, the continuity of the experiential, is the source of the collective health of the nation and the psychological well being of its individual members.

When *Haratch* is over, one senses a resolution absent in the previous plays. As the individual recognizes his or her role in, and accepts responsibility for, the act of self and community creation, the solution of problems for both the *I* and the *we* can have said to have begun.

This trilogy of plays about Armenians exposes William Saroyan's affinity to ancestral origins differently from either the early Armenian stories, which are usually descriptive rather than analytic, or novels like *Rock Wagram*. They are perhaps even more revealing of a commitment to things Armenian than the already published correspondence with Armenian writers and editors or his various prefaces for books by others about Armenians. The grace of art, and the transformational magic of theater, achieved in these plays through Saroyan's absolute command of dramatic dialogue, make them eloquently complex and universal statements about that part of his personal heritage still hardly known and poorly understood even by those close to him. For critic and biographer, the circumstance of genocide and exile, the exotic facts of Armenian history, are more difficult to negotiate than the more popular currency of social and psychological analysis. Aram Saroyan, for instance, in both the biographical memoir *Last Rites* and the biography *William Saroyan*, interprets his father's emotional problems exclusively through a Freudian examination of the consequences of Armenak's death on his three year-old son, followed by five years' residency in an orphanage. No one who has read Saroyan can ignore the importance of the loss of father to the writer. But who has yet spoken of or tried to measure the effects of loss of fatherland on Saroyan's life and work? This deprivation, caused by the trauma of the Genocide, has disturbed every Armenian writer of the century, just as the Holocaust has not escaped the conscience of any contemporary Jewish writer. Certainly its effect on Saroyan was deep and constant, the source of many of his most characteristic traits and attitudes. *Armenians*, *Bitlis*, and *Haratch* display the power of national environment on the artist, his imagination, and, by extrapolation, his creative urges. Until the internal landscape of these plays is grasped, studied, and appreciated, any biography of Saroyan will be perforce incomplete.

Outside the public's eye, in the last decade of a half century of writing, Saroyan, with his pervasive literary humor and bonhommie, was able through these plays to engage seriously the disorienting dilemmas associated with living in an unwanted diaspora. While the accumulated frustration of national exile caused by a terrifying genocide—one nearly forgotten and even denied by its perpetrators—drove some to the desperation of violence, it motivated Saroyan to demand of himself clarifications of this confounding experience, clarifications articulated through art. He tries to show in the plays that the agonizing frustration of endlessly waiting for a better, more just future can only be overcome with the freedom gained by the willful affirmation of each individual to be a conscious part of the disinherited collectivity.

Finally, one may ask whether these at times metaphysical plays were intended for the stage or were just essays in dialogue form? There is no doubt in the case of *Armenians* considering Saroyan's personal initiative in offering the play and preparing program notes for the premier. But what about *Bitlis* and especially *Haratch*? Not only do they totally lack stage directions, like all the later plays, but there is hardly any action: everyone is sitting around talking. Some critics were bewildered by *The Time of Your Life*, claiming that nothing happened even though the stage was peopled with singers, dancers, and an endless procession of minor figures. Saroyan was against theater dependent on excessive stage action, emotionality, and hyper-dramatic endings. He found violence a bogus trick for capturing audience attention, and said so publicly numerous times. Yet these works should not deceive by the ease of their language or their humor; they are serious dramas whose purpose is to portray universal experience through individual manifestations of it. Saroyan wanted his characters to talk about vital things, intelligently, and compassionately, or at least interestingly, to each other and thereby to the audience and to the world.

These plays are not just dialogues, intellectual exercises, or Saroyan's journals put in dramatic form. They are theatrical pieces intended for the stage. Like every one of his plays, they are a challenge to the skill of the most talented directors because of the problems and paradoxes they seek to unravel. Their intensity and brilliance is not defined by action or plot, but by language and idea. Their message is universal and enduring.

ARMENIANS

A Play in Two Acts

The play opens in Holy Trinity Armenian Apostolic Church on the corner of Ventura and M in Fresno. The church was designed and built by architect Lawrence Cone (Kondrakian) between 1912 and 1914. The photo above was taken shortly after its completion. (Photo courtesy of Mrs. L. Cone and Robby Antoyan) Below, the church in 1985 as seen from the parking lot of the new Holiday Inn erected on the site of the Asbarez Patriotic Club where the second part of the play takes place. (Photo Aram Messerlian, CSUF Armenian Studies Archive)

Above, the priest of Holy Trinity, Fr. Kasparian in 1912, shortly after his arrival in Fresno from Bursa, Turkey with Deacon Paul Vartenian and students of the Armenian School of the church. (Photo courtesy of Allan Jendian) Below, Archbishop Kasparian in his later years. (Photo courtesy of Fr. Vartan Kasparian, Yettem, California)

Saroyan and his family were members of the First Armenian Presbyterian Church on Fulton Street in Fresno, built in 1901 and used until 1941. (Photo courtesy of First Armenian Presbyterian Church)

Reverend Muggerditch H. Knadjian, spiritual head of the First Armenian Presbyterian Church from 1912 to 1920. (Photo courtesy of the First Armenian Presbyterian Church.) Below, the original First Presyterian building still stands as a Fresno County historical landmark with the name The Fulton House. It is this structure, used today for public gatherings and ceremonies, that Saroyan once considered buying. (Photo Aram Messerlian, CSUF Armenian Studies Archive)

Pilgrim Armenian Congregational Church, Fresno, the first building on Van Ness and Inyo, used from 1910 to 1921. (Photo courtesy of Pilgrim Armenian Congregational Church)

Reverend M. G. Papazian, Resident Minister of the Pilgrim Armenian Congregational Church from 1914 to 1940. Below, the second Pilgrim Church building on M and Merced Streets, used from 1921, the year of the action of *Armenians*, to 1961. (Photos courtesy of the Pilgrim Armenian Congregational Church)

The poster of the premier production of *Armenians* directed by Ed Setrakian in New York, October 1974.

Two scenes from the New York production of *Armenians*, October 1974: above, Fr. Kasparian, played by Director Ed Setrakian, helps Rev. Papazian, played by Luis Avalos; below, Joseph Ragno as Dr. Jivelekian with the Man from Moush. (Photos after *The Armenian Church*, December 1974)

Armenians was produced by the Diocese of the Armenian Church of America in the Haig Kavookjian Armenian Arts Center, 630 Second Avenue in New York City on October 22, 23, 24, 29, 30, 31 and November 11, 12, 13, 14, 1974. It was directed by Ed Setrakian. The Equity Approved Showcase performances featured the following cast:

FATHER KASPARIAN	Ed Setrakian
REVEREND MUGGERDITCH KNADJIAN	Warren Finnerty
REVEREND PAPAZIAN	Luis Avalos
ALMAST	Terese Hayden
SEXTON	Nicholas Daddazio
DOCTOR ARSHAK JIVELEKIAN	Joseph Ragno
FARMER	Murray Moston
MAN FROM BITLIS	Vahagn Hovannes
MAN FROM MOUSH	Raymond Cole
MAN FROM VAN	Harold Cherry
MAN FROM HARPOOT	David Patch
VASKEN	Bob Doran
MAN FROM ERZEROUM	Rudy Bond
MAN FROM DIKRANAGERT	Sal Carollo
MAN FROM GILIGIA	Robert Coluntino

The technical staff included:

Stage Manager	Susan Gregg
Production Coordinator	Alice Eminian
Sets and Lights	John Brennan, Eric Cowley, Torkom Demirjian, Bob Doran
Costumes	Ruth Thomason
Props	Anne Setrakian

The following Program Note was prepared by the author for the premier production:

Program Note

The play called *Armenians* is about people. The time of the play is approximately yesterday, 1921. At that time the playwright was thirteen years old, and pretty much fascinated by everything that he saw in the streets and places of Fresno, California, which he visited daily in the course of his work as a newsboy—not a route carrier, that's another kind of connection with newspapers, but a seller of papers, a walker, a headline-shouter, a visitor of places, an observer of people.

Some of the playwright's observations of some of the people of Fresno are in this play, from both before 1921 and from long after, including this morning when a man outside a dentist's door said, You are not what I expected you to be.

I said, Well, I can't say I'm sorry because I don't know what you expected, or why. Do you speak Armenian?

He then said in Armenian, I expected you to be *shavlar*, or something like that, which he said was the proper Armenian word for fat.

I replied in Armenian, Oh, I thought your disappointment was the consequence of having read my books and then many years later finding me coarse and common in comparison with them. (You should have heard me in Armenian. It was really elegant.)

No, he said, from photographs in papers and from friends who know you.

And these friends of yours, I said, where are they now?

Well, he said, home, or dead. I myself am eighty-two years old and had a stroke two years ago.

How many children have you? I said, and he said, Well I married this Pennsylvania Dutch woman who is in the dentist's chair right now and we don't have any children.

Well, the man's dying, you see, and he hasn't left any fighters in the world, half Armenian and half Pennsylvania Dutch. Of course this compels regret in me because while Armenians have in America married into all races there is enough of Armenia in their kids to keep the old fight going, and so here this morning was this good man at death's door with his wife in the dentist's chair and no kids at all, and therefore no grandkids who, like as not, would be only one-quarter Armenian.

I tried not to show my astonishment and disappointment, but soon enough got back on my bike and rode off, wishing him good luck, although I can't imagine where.

This play is a little bit about that sort of thing, if in an indirect way.

In wanting ourselves continued in the fight of the world, what we really want is the continuance of the human family itself, in its broadest, deepest, most complex, most troublesome, most unaccountable, most unacceptable, most preposterous, most contradictory, and most inexhaustibly unpredictable reality.

But what for?

Why?

For the reason that only out of that awful but also magnificent *fullness* may we expect the human race to begin—*to begin*, mark you— to become the fulfillment of what has been indicated in his nature and truth for as long as there has been a chronicle of such things—chiselled in stone, painted on cave walls, put up into breathtaking architecture, murmured in lullabies, whispered and roared in symphonies, held fast and secret inside all invented shapes—ship, locomotive, airplane, phonographs, radio, television (for instance). But probably even more significantly in the *model* of all shapes, the egg, which of course eludes us entirely, having come as we ourselves have come, from the soul and heart of secrecy itself.

We certainly want everybody to continue in the fight, and that of course has got to include the Turk, may his eyes open into the privilege and helplessness which is the mark of humanity.

The play *Armenians* perhaps says, It's hopeless and we know it, but not so hopeless we don't want to find out how hopeless it is.

Fresno, California
October 18, 1974

WILLIAM SAROYAN

THE PEOPLE

FATHER KASPARIAN, *priest of the Red Brick Armenian Apostolic Church*

REVEREND MUGGERDITCH KNADJIAN, *48, minister of First Armenian Presbyterian Church*

REVEREND PAPAZIAN, *44, minister of Pilgrim Armenian Congregational Church*

ALMAST, *octogenarian woman from Moush, helper to Fr. Kasparian*

SEXTON, *of the Red Brick Church, Markar by name*

DOCTOR ARSHAK JIVELEKIAN, *58, from Boston, educated at Harvard*

FARMER, *74 years old*

MAN FROM BITLIS

MAN FROM MOUSH, *Baghdasar Der Kaprielian by name*

MAN FROM VAN

MAN FROM HARPOOT, *Giragos Arpiar Der Havasarian, oriental rug seller*

VASKEN, *a man from Harpoot*

MAN FROM ERZEROUM

MAN FROM DIKRANAGERT

MAN FROM GILIGIA

THE PLACE

The Office of the Red Brick Church (Holy Trinity Armenian Apostolic Church) on the corner of Ventura at M Street, Fresno, California.

The Armenian Patriotic Club facing the church on Ventura.

THE TIME

A morning in the Spring of 1921.

NOTE. The play was written in one act with twenty-one scenes in Fresno between November 10 and 30, 1971. The New York production divided it into two acts corresponding to the natural change of setting. The two act arrangement has been retained by the editor.

ACT ONE

PAPAZIAN, KASPARIAN, KNADJIAN in the office of the Red Brick Church on Ventura at M Street in Fresno, 1921.

Slowly, easily, thoughtfully, with considerings of what has been said until the KEY is established and the reality is being supported by the audience.

KASPARIAN.   I trust we may all stand rather than sit.

KNADJIAN.   I prefer to stand, also.

PAPAZIAN.   Perhaps you will not mind if I relieve the pain in my right ankle by taking this chair.

KASPARIAN.   A sip of cognac is surely in order.

PAPAZIAN.   No thank you, I do not drink.

KASPARIAN.   And you?

KNADJIAN.   On occasion.

KASPARIAN.   Let this be such an occasion. My hours are long. I have been up since before daybreak.

KNADJIAN.   May I propose that we drink to harmony among all of us.

KASPARIAN.   Very well, harmony, then. Ah, that was good. Another?

KNADJIAN.   Very good, but no more for me, thank you.

KASPARIAN.   This second sip for me, and now, who will speak first?

PAPAZIAN.   Let us be good Americans first, and then Armenians.

KASPARIAN.   Good or bad?

PAPAZIAN.   If we are good Americans, we will be good Armenians, as well.

KNADJIAN.   My church has always felt close to the Mother Church.

PAPAZIAN.   We are certainly all Christians. Our disputes are not religious, they are political.

KASPARIAN.   Is it political to pray that Armenia will continue to be an independent nation?

PAPAZIAN.   *Was* an independent nation. Perhaps you have not seen this morning's *Examiner* from San Francisco. Independent Armenia is now a part of the New Russia.

KASPARIAN.   I was informed by telephone from New York last night. The Russian invaders were driven off once before.

PAPAZIAN.   I don't know what to say. The suffering of the people who are there must be beyond imagining. Hunger, cold, homelessness, fear, pain, sickness, madness, despair. Isn't it enough?

KASPARIAN. There will be more—much more, I'm afraid—whether Armenia is free or part of Russia. You seem distressed.

KNADJIAN. I am. I had heard rumors of this tragic development but I hoped....

PAPAZIAN. Not tragic. It may be our salvation.

KNADJIAN. How? Please tell me how?

KASPARIAN. Let us agree not to argue, at any rate. We haven't got that much time. Let us also agree that we shall be very patient about our people in the home country, and very helpful to our people right here. There is the matter of our boys and girls growing up unable to read and write Armenian. And many marry members of other nationalities. And of course many of our young people either refuse to come to this church, or even to your church, or to yours, and if they do come, they are bored, and they even tell jokes to one another during the services.

PAPAZIAN. Yes, it is true. What shall we do?

KASPARIAN. We must work on the parents. If they do not teach their children to be Armenian, we can do nothing to improve the situation.

KNADJIAN. My wife is an Englishwoman, and so my children are only half-Armenian. I must confess I have not been able to make them love Armenia.

PAPAZIAN. And that is precisely how it is with me, too.

KASPARIAN. Well, forget your own children, then, but do not forget the children of Armenia, itself. And now I must say good-day, gentlemen.

PAPAZIAN. Let me sit a little longer, and then help me up, please.

KNADJIAN. As you say. Is it really a condition, or did you make a point of sitting in his presence because of his robes and the difference between his Christianity and yours?

PAPAZIAN. His Christianity is quite all right, it's his air of authority I find a little unacceptable. He thinks we are fools.

KNADJIAN. I frequently think so, too.

PAPAZIAN. Think for yourself. I don't think I am a fool at all. The Americans respect me.

KNADJIAN. Well, of course Father Kasparian doesn't speak English, so the Americans don't know him.

PAPAZIAN. They know he doesn't speak English. He has no right not to learn to speak English.

KNADJIAN. But your ankle, is it sprained or what?

PAPAZIAN. It is nothing, but I will not do the bidding of a man who believes the strange things that that man believes.

KNADJIAN. Christianity?

PAPAZIAN. No, I'm thinking of his politics.

KNADJIAN. I rather admire his politics. He does not want Armenia to disappear from the face of the earth. He believes it is important for Armenians to maintain their identity.

PAPAZIAN. That is a decision for God to make.

KNADJIAN. He wants to help God.

PAPAZIAN. That is not necessary.

KNADJIAN. I have always believed it is the one thing that is always necessary, but never mind, will you get up now?

PAPAZIAN. A moment longer. Where did he go so abruptly?

KNADJIAN. Oh, he has chores of many kinds, both ecclesiastical and secular. I believe he is making house calls this morning.

PAPAZIAN. What in the world for?

KNADJIAN. The sexton was speaking of it to an old friend when we came in. The old friend's wife is dying, and the sexton said, He will go with you in a moment. Didn't you notice? Didn't you hear? We stood there together.

PAPAZIAN. I was deep in thought. I noticed nothing, heard nothing.

KNADJIAN. Well, then, take my hand, I'll help you up. I must return to my study.

PAPAZIAN. What do you do when you go to your study? Sleep?

KNADJIAN. Oh, no. Plenty of time to sleep, at home. I wouldn't think of sleeping when I am in my study, the place I love best in this whole world.

PAPAZIAN. Is that so? Why?

KNADJIAN. I find that I am most myself there, I am most real there, I am most deeply Armenian when I am in my study. And of course I proceed with my work.

PAPAZIAN. Church work? You prepare your next sermon?

KNADJIAN. That, too, but I prefer to *make up* my sermon as I go along. When I am in my study my work is to write.

PAPAZIAN. What do you write? Love lyrics. So many preachers are secretly very amorous—at least in the head.

KNADJIAN. No, I write history. Well, at any rate I write what I have experienced, what I remember, what I was told, what I have felt, and of course I also invent out of these things a kind of truth which I think is greater than factual truth.

PAPAZIAN.   And what truth is that?

KNADJIAN.   Creative truth. The truth of art. Of passion of mind and spirit. Armenian truth.

PAPAZIAN.   Are you all that Armenian?

KNADJIAN.   Yes, I am. And you?

PAPAZIAN.   I'm not sure. Sometimes I believe I am more English, but in the end, it seems, I am no such thing. I am only Armenian.

KNADJIAN.   Only? Do you think there is something better to be?

PAPAZIAN.   Possibly.

KASPARIAN.   Gentlemen, are you still here?

PAPAZIAN.   Alas, my ankle pains me.

KASPARIAN.   Shall I have somebody telephone for an ambulance?

PAPAZIAN.   Oh, no no, I will be all right.

KASPARIAN.   Then, shall I have the woman bring tea. I take tea now, before I go back to work.

KNADJIAN.   I think a cup of tea will be just fine, and it will give me an opportunity to say that I am in deep sorrow about conditions in Armenia.

PAPAZIAN.   And so am I, but we must not make them worse. The people have suffered enough. Let us be patient.

KASPARIAN.   Perhaps, but not for tea. Almast, please pour for three.

KNADJIAN.   And who is Almast?

KASPARIAN.   A woman of the neighborhood, who helps with such things.

PAPAZIAN.   Isn't the name Kurdish? Almast?

KASPARIAN.   The woman is Armenian—from Moush.

PAPAZIAN.   In my congregation there are no people from Moush.

KASPARIAN.   They are devoted to the true church, which as you know is Armenia itself. Here's tea, then. Help yourselves to sugar and lemon. Almast, these are the pastors of the Congregational Church, and of the Presbyterian Church.

ALMAST.   Do you really believe?

PAPAZIAN.   Of course we do. We are Christians, just as you are.

ALMAST.   That's good. Then, believe, and perhaps all will be well.

KNADJIAN.   Yes, yes, in time all will be well.

ALMAST.   We shall all die, but before we do perhaps all will be well.

PAPAZIAN.   Thank you, thank you.

KASPARIAN.   She is more than eighty years old, but still as alive as a young woman.

KNADJIAN.   And she has a very strong mind.

KASPARIAN.   The mind of a woman of Moush.

PAPAZIAN.   Come to think of it, you yourself are from Moush, are you not?

KASPARIAN.   I am.

PAPAZIAN.   A villager.

KASPARIAN.   Yes, and you?

PAPAZIAN.   I am from Aintab, but I studied in Istanbul, one of the leading cities of the world.

KASPARIAN.   I only saw it once, from the deck of a ship, but I have never been there. And you?

KNADJIAN.   I am from Marsovan.

KASPARIAN.   I passed through Marsovan. My friends, the church in our country was the nation itself until the arrival of the missionaries. I do not know why you two became students at the missionary schools, but I am sure your reasons were sensible. They were the best schools with the best teachers, and in addition to everything else you studied and learned English.

PAPAZIAN.   Also French, and a little German.

KASPARIAN.   I read and write and speak only Armenian, as you know. I met all of the missionaries in Moush as a boy and I found them strangely unacceptable. They were Christian but they were not Armenian, that was what made the difference. And you are Christian, but you have each of you lost a little of that part of yourselves which was entirely Armenian.

PAPAZIAN.   We are men of the world. The Christian world, of course.

KASPARIAN.   That is true. I have heard about the sermons you have given in the English language, which have been heard by many Americans.

KNADJIAN.   Since we are in dispersion it is desirable and necessary for us to become members of the society in which we find ourselves.

KASPARIAN.   No doubt, but do you forget Armenia instantly? Can't you wait just a little? Give us a little time?

KNADJIAN.   We need at least twenty years.

PAPAZIAN.   At the very least ten.

KASPARIAN.   No, gentlemen, we need a hundred years, at least.

PAPAZIAN. Let me thank you for asking us to come and visit, and also for this excellent tea. What kind is it?

KASPARIAN. I wanted to see you both, I wanted to have you see me, I wanted to exchange a few words with you, I wanted to find out if there is anything that we may expect from either of you.

PAPAZIAN. And the tea?

KASPARIAN. It is tea from the store. Lipton's. Ten cents. But Almast adds cloves and cinnamon and other things.

KNADJIAN. And I thank you for having me come to visit. As for the matter of what we may expect from one another, that is indeed something we are eager to learn—all of us, all our lives, but I wonder, do we ever learn, do we ever really find out?

PAPAZIAN. I expect from you a continuation of your traditional ecclesiastical procedures, in accordance with your training and the expectations of your congregation. Perhaps you will accept that volunteered statement, and then perhaps you will tell me what you expect of me.

KASPARIAN. Yes, that is only fair, but the expectation I am thinking of is not quite so superficial. Of course I shall do my work as I have been trained to do it, and you shall do yours as you have been trained, but there are other areas of expectation that I am concerned about.

KNADJIAN. What may we expect of one another not as men of God, if I may put it that way, but as men of the world, of the human race, of the nation, of the family?

KASPARIAN. Yes, that is coming nearer to the expectation I am thinking of.

PAPAZIAN. As a man I believe I may be counted on to take a neutral stand in all matters of politics.

KASPARIAN. Well, that is certainly a clear statement, but do you really believe it is possible for any man, let alone a man who gives guidance and instruction to hundreds of other men, to be neutral. Is there such a thing as neutrality?

PAPAZIAN. I believe there is. For instance, I am aware that you do not cherish the arrival of the Russians into the life of the new Armenian nation. I believe you have a perfect right to that feeling. Isn't that neutrality?

KASPARIAN. I don't know, but whatever neutrality is, it is not very useful to anybody, and time is running out, if we do not do useful things whenever it is possible or necessary to do them, we shall soon be totally departed from the human scene, and forgotten, or remembered only for having disappeared. Armenians are too vital to be permitted to throw themselves away in neutrality, comfort, well-being, satisfaction, and so on and so forth.

KNADJIAN. I believe I understand what you are saying. Please tell me what you would like to expect from both of us, or each of us, one at a time. What can I do for Armenia? We are nine thousand miles away from Armenia, and the Russians are *there*, what can I do at the First Armenian Presbyterian Church of Fresno, at Santa Clara and J Street?

KASPARIAN. Yes, you have every right to ask me, to ask yourself, to ask him that question. You can do precisely what you are obliged to do in the conduct of your duties, but you can add to all of that the powerful belief that Armenia, although occupied by the Russians, *is* Armenian, not Russian, and that the Armenian people will become more and more Armenian with time passing and more experience and wisdom of the world coming to them, and that furthermore Armenians in dispersion all over the world, but especially here in California, in Fresno, will continue to be Armenians, they will not become so foolishly American that being also Armenian will even be an embarrassment to them, and something to forget as quickly as possible, by marrying foreigners and bringing up children who neither know nor care that they are Armenians.

PAPAZIAN. I can't understand your excitement. It makes you say things that I'm not sure make sense.

KNADJIAN. I'm sure you do understand, for I do, and we both have children who are not interested in being Armenians.

SEXTON. Father, have you forgotten? They're waiting.

KASPARIAN. Ah, thank you, Markar. The funeral, is that correct?

SEXTON. No, Father. This is a baptism.

KASPARIAN. A boy or a girl?

SEXTON. Two boys, twins.

KASPARIAN. We don't often have twins.

SEXTON. The father is Irish, it's the mother who is Armenian.

KASPARIAN. And the father wants his sons baptised in the Armenian church?

SEXTON. He insists on it.

KASPARIAN. Who is this man?

SEXTON. The name is Michael Higgins. He will be able to say a few words to you in the Armenian language.

KASPARIAN. That is very interesting, I must say. And the mother, who is she?

SEXTON. Alice Bashbanian.

KASPARIAN. Bashban. Alice Bashbanian. And what are the names of the boys? Michael? Patrick? Something like that?

SEXTON. No, Father. Aram. Dikran.

KASPARIAN. Amazing. Aram Higgins. Dikran Higgins. It has a strange ring to it. Gentlemen, please keep your places, enjoy the tea, if you want anything, I will send Almast. Do not go. Wait for my return.

KNADJIAN. May I be present at the baptism?

KASPARIAN. Of course. I'm sure you know the ritual.

KNADJIAN. Yes, and I use it now and then.

PAPAZIAN. Please forgive me if I remain seated. My ankle.

KASPARIAN. Rest easy. Oh, Almast, please ask Reverend Papazian to have more tea and cakes.

ALMAST. Please let me fill your cup, and please have another cake.

PAPAZIAN. Thank you, and how long have you been serving the good Father?

ALMAST. Oh, just these few years. I have nobody now, these few years.

PAPAZIAN. Something happened? A loss?

ALMAST. Yes, several losses.

PAPAZIAN. If it is not too painful, perhaps you won't mind telling me about them.

ALMAST. They have all died. They were all killed.

PAPAZIAN. During these past few years? Who was it? Where did it happen?

ALMAST. Well, it was all of them. I am alone, except for the good Father, and the other people who come to the church.

PAPAZIAN. Being alone is sometimes a good thing, but it is also a very bad thing. I hope you have become at home within yourself, alone.

ALMAST. No, that has not happened. It is now six years since I lost them all, but I have not become at home within myself.

PAPAZIAN. You have God.

ALMAST. Yes, He is here in the church, always.

PAPAZIAN. And you have Jesus.

ALMAST. Well, I don't know about Jesus. I know we say we have Jesus, but I don't know. I know we have God, but I don't know Jesus, I really have no experience of Jesus.

PAPAZIAN. We are Christians, of course you have Jesus.

ALMAST. Yes, sir, if you say so.

PAPAZIAN. Our whole nation has Jesus.

ALMAST. Our nation is lost, and I lost all of my family in our loss of the nation. I do not blame Jesus, but I don't know if He has ever helped us.

PAPAZIAN. What you say is very strange for an Armenian. It was for Jesus that so many of us died.

ALMAST. But *we* did not, you and I, did we? Perhaps we don't care for Jesus very much.

PAPAZIAN. You are a very strange woman, I must say.

ALMAST. The good Father does not think so. We have talked about this many times, and he has never said that I am very strange.

KASPARIAN. Well now how is your foot?

PAPAZIAN. Better, thank you, Father, but it is not my foot, it is my ankle.

KNADJIAN. You should have seen the twins. One is blonde with blue eyes, the other is black haired with dark eyes—but they are brothers.

PAPAZIAN. I had a very interesting chat with your housekeeper, Father.

KASPARIAN. Will you have a drop? I need a drop.

PAPAZIAN. No, Father, thank you very much. I do not drink.

KASPARIAN. It might do your foot good.

PAPAZIAN. But they say alcoholic beverages are the very *cause* of gout.

KASPARIAN. Your gout is caused by something else, perhaps a drop will cure it—at least for a moment.

PAPAZIAN. The point is, I don't believe Almast is a Christian.

KASPARIAN. She is a woman, and a good woman.

PAPAZIAN. But this is a Christian church.

KASPARIAN. And Almast is a very important part of this church.

PAPAZIAN. But she doesn't believe in Jesus.

KNADJIAN. Take a sip of this fine *rakhi*, it will do you good.

PAPAZIAN. I do not believe in the use of alcoholic beverages under any circumstances.

KNADJIAN. Take a sip *without* believing.

PAPAZIAN. That is not possible for me. Is it possible for you?

KNADJIAN. Yes, I accept certain things without knowing very much about them.

PAPAZIAN. Such as? Are you speaking in riddles, parables, and proverbs?

KNADJIAN. Oh, no. But I don't know very much about anything, and yet I *have* everything that I have in this kind of ignorance and faith.

PAPAZIAN. I like to know what I have and what I don't have, and why.

KASPARIAN. I am renewed.

PAPAZIAN. By the alcohol? Is that what you are saying?

KASPARIAN. By the variety that is in as few as three or four people. The inexhaustible variety of the human race. Of the Armenians. Of one family of Armenians. And perhaps by the inexhaustible variety in only one Armenian.

PAPAZIAN. Which Armenian is that?

KASPARIAN. Any Armenian. Yourself, for instance.

PAPAZIAN. I am consistent, and uncontradictory, there is no variety in me.

KASPARIAN. Perhaps, or is it that you don't know about yourself, your consistency, your contradictions, and your variety.

PAPAZIAN. I am a steadfast Christian. But that is an established fact. The whole world knows that. I share the pulpits of many churches in this city. I am written about in both of the daily newspapers.

KASPARIAN. I have heard. What do you *say* in your sermons?

PAPAZIAN. Well, of course that depends on the topic, doesn't it? On Mother's Day I speak of mothers. On Father's Day I speak of fathers. I tell the world to be like Jesus.

KASPARIAN. Yes, that is a good thing to tell anybody. Again, I must tear myself away from such good company and such good talk. Almast is here to remind me of my next chore.

ALMAST. This is an emergency. Akob Dudu's dying. She wants you to give her the last rites. Her granddaughter has come to fetch you. The little girl will take you to their house. It isn't far.

KASPARIAN. Very well, and thank you, gentlemen. Please come again and let us continue our discussions.

KNADJIAN. Thank you, Father, but I hesitate to intrude and take up your valuable time.

KASPARIAN. No, no, come any time you like, if I'm not here, I will be soon enough. And you, be sure you come here any time you like. I enjoy our talks.

PAPAZIAN. I don't seem to make any impression on you, however. You don't seem to mind at all if somebody who works in your church is not even a Christian.

KASPARIAN. I mind, but I mind other things, too. Good day, gentlemen.

KNADJIAN. Then, let me help you to your feet, and back to your church.

PAPAZIAN. Do you have a carriage, to take me?

KNADJIAN. No, but I can support you as we walk. It's only four blocks. In the old country we ran four miles as if it were nothing.

PAPAZIAN. This is not the old country, and we are no longer boys, we are men, and old men at that.

KNADJIAN. I do not consider myself an old man. But up, now, lean on me, up, what's the matter with your ankle?

PAPAZIAN. Both of my ankles have gone bad. First one and then the other. I don't know what it is. I am forty-four years old, is that your age, also?

KNADJIAN. I see, I see. I am even older than you, I am forty-eight, and I do not consider myself an old man, at all, I consider myself nearer to boyhood than to senility. Why should your ankles go bad?

PAPAZIAN. I wish I knew. I really wish I knew.

KNADJIAN. And your doctor, what does he say? You have gone to a doctor, I presume. A man of your character does not neglect bad ankles. An Armenian doctor, because when a man is in pain he likes to speak the family language.

PAPAZIAN. Yes, yes, your understanding is quite good. I went first to the Americans—to three different doctors, the most famous ones—and then I went to the old Armenian.

KNADJIAN. Jivvy?

PAPAZIAN. Do you call him Jivvy?

KNADJIAN. Jivelekian is an old friend, and we have always spoken to one another as if we were still boys in the old country. He calls me Mugo, for Muggerditch of course. Jivvy is not only a good doctor he is a good man. And what did he prescribe to relieve the pain?

PAPAZIAN.   He didn't prescribe anything. Ah, well, how shall I put it. He told me to pray. Imagine the impertinence of such a suggestion. Praying is my profession, medicine is his. I went to him for medical help, he turns around and tells me to get ecclesiastical help. He tells me to pray.

KNADJIAN.   Jivvy's very wise.

PAPAZIAN.   Well, of course I did not let him know I was annoyed. After all, I consider myself a man of some refinement.

KNADJIAN.   Speak of the devil. Dr. Jivelekian, what are you doing *here*?

JIVELEKIAN.   Gentlemen, gentlemen. The priest sent for me. It seems somebody is dying. Where is the priest?

PAPAZIAN.   He's gone to the dying woman's bedside. Look here, Dr. Jivelekian, my ankles are making a terrible fool of me. Surely there are pills I can take to restore the ankles to their proper strength.

JIVELEKIAN.   Aspirin. I suggest aspirin to everybody, for everything. Are you taking aspirin?

PAPAZIAN.   No, Doctor. Aspirin is for headaches. It is my ankles that hurt.

JIVELEKIAN.   Take two aspirin every time you remember that your ankles hurt. Before you know it they won't hurt any more. Your feet and your ankles and your legs, and for that matter your whole body seems to be quite sound. A couple of aspirin now and then is all you really need. Who is dying?

PAPAZIAN.   An old woman. An old woman.

JIVELEKIAN.   Well, I must get to her. Who is she? Where is she?

KNADJIAN.   Akob Dudu. Do you know where she lives?

JIVELEKIAN.   Yes, of course, I've been there many times.

PAPAZIAN.   Poor woman.

KNADJIAN.   Why are you sitting down, Dr. Jivelekian?

JIVELEKIAN.   I can't help her.

KNADJIAN.   What is her illness?

JIVELEKIAN.   I don't know. The same as the good Reverend's ankle trouble. Who knows?

KNADJIAN.   Let us go across the street to the Patriotic Club and have a small coffee apiece. Here, hold onto me, you'll be all right.

PAPAZIAN.   Thank you, thank you, friendship is a fine thing.

JIVELEKIAN.   And a game of cards, too. Agreed, Mugo?

KNADJIAN.   Agreed, Jivvy.

ACT TWO

*The Armenian Patriotic Club on Ventura Street opposite the Red
Brick Church.*

KNADJIAN. Dr. Jivelekian, are you sure we should be sitting here in
the Patriotic Club sipping coffee?

JIVELEKIAN. Of course I'm sure. Why do you ask?

KNADJIAN. I find that I have great anxiety about the old woman,
Akob Dudu. Perhaps you and I, who have good ankles, ought to
get up from this table immediately and hurry to her house, where
the good Father is, and do what we can for the old lady.

JIVELEKIAN. Forget it. I have been to Akob Dudu's house a dozen
times so far this year. She is just fine.

PAPAZIAN. But you said you couldn't help her. How can she be just
fine?

JIVELEKIAN. She's eighty-eight years old. Little things go wrong with
her all the time. My visits improve the day for her, a little, I suppose.
The last time I was there, day before yesterday, she was bored,
that's all.

PAPAZIAN. Doctor, I hesitate to say this, but it seems to me that now
more than ever, you of all people, should go to the old woman and
keep her company. I would go except for my ankles, but my being
with her couldn't mean anything much, considering Father Kasparian
is there, and he will attend to the needs of her immortal soul, but
you are needed, for you attend to the needs of her body. It is your
duty to go to the old woman.

JIVELEKIAN. I suppose it is in a way, but I am afraid I am not going
to do my duty today. I'm going to sit here and enjoy this coffee
and then a game of cards—will you play, Reverend Papazian?

PAPAZIAN. Cards? Oh, no, no, no, no, no, no. Look at all of these
unfortunate men in this Patriotic Club, all of them past fifty, all
of them able-bodied, and all of them idle. Idleness is very dangerous.
It leads to trouble. They should be out in the world doing good
works.

KNADJIAN. I believe they *were* out in the world and they have done
their good works for the year, now it is time to rest. The season's
over, the crops are harvested, the year's rewards have been received,
the interest on the bank loans have been made, clothes have been

bought for the children, so they can look well at school, and so these good farmers are enjoying a well-earned rest.

PAPAZIAN. Farmers? They are not all farmers, only one or two are farmers, the rest are loafers, that's what they are. Useless men. They produce nothing.

KNADJIAN. There isn't one man in this place who hasn't produced children.

JIVELEKIAN. And I have brought into the world about half of those children. All healthy, too, I might say. Let the boys have their innocent fun.

PAPAZIAN. But is it innocent? Is idleness ever innocent?

JIVELEKIAN. They are not idle. They are busy concentrating on the card games, or the backgammon games, or the reading of the coffee grounds in their cups, or the news from Armenia. Well, what is it now?

KNADJIAN. For the second time in a year the Russians have taken over Armenia.

JIVELEKIAN. Is that so? And if it is so, and there is nothng we can do about it, what shall we do?

PAPAZIAN. Nothing. That is the wisest course in such political matters. Let time make some sense out of the wrongs and rights.

JIVELEKIAN. Yes, there is something to that. Be patient and something will happen.

KNADJIAN. In the meantime, are we entitled to forget that members of the Armenian government have been placed in jail and some of them have been shot, and others will be jailed and shot? That is the question.

PAPAZIAN. How can we help them? Did we do anything to have them jailed or shot?

KNADJIAN. No, I only mean, this is something to think about, at least.

JIVELEKIAN. If you want to know the truth, any time I can't sleep I find that I am thinking about our *intellectuals* jailed and shot. I don't like it.

PAPAZIAN. Of course not. What do you see in your coffee grounds?

JIVELEKIAN. Mountains and meadows and rivers—Armenia. It makes me angry.

KNADJIAN. Well, shuffle the cards and let's have a game, shall we?

JIVELEKIAN. We shall, we shall indeed.

FARMER. Dr. Jivelekian, excuse me.

JIVELEKIAN. Yes, what is it?

FARMER. Can I speak to you a moment?

JIVELEKIAN. Yes, go right ahead, just speak.

FARMER. My back hurts.

JIVELEKIAN. What have you done in the way of work to make it hurt?

FARMER. Well, of course I've been loading heavy boxes of raisins onto wagons for taking to the packing house.

JIVELEKIAN. How heavy?

FARMER. Well, the small boxes are eighty pounds, but the big boxes are two hundred, and two men lift the big boxes.

JIVELEKIAN. Rest your back, it will be all right.

FARMER. It hurts.

JIVELEKIAN. I'm here for a little recreation, in the form of a card game. If you want to go into the matter more extensively, go to my office at two o'clock this afternoon.

FARMER. Your office? If I go to your office, you will charge me a dollar, we are countrymen, how can you be so mercenary?

JIVELEKIAN. Go to my office, and I promise, I will charge you nothing. I want to finish this game of *scambile*.

FARMER. But if I go to your office I will have to leave the backgammon tournament, and I'm winning.

JIVELEKIAN. Well what do you want me to do? I'm perfectly willing to be as patriotic as possible. Your back hurts. You've been lifting heavy boxes, so of course it hurts. I've told you, rest your back. You are not satisfied with that. What will make you happy, sir?

FARMER. I'm seventy-four years old. I thought you would want to study my back.

JIVELEKIAN. Very well. Turn around. There you are. Your back is very strong. You've strained the muscles a little from doing heavy work, but if you avoid such work, your back will be just fine again very soon. I'm fifty-eight years old.

FARMER. Suppose I get into a hot tub tonight before bedtime? Will that help?

JIVELEKIAN. Yes, it will.

FARMER. And what are we going to do about the news from Armenia?

JIVELEKIAN. Is your back all right, now?

FARMER. The Russians have taken the country again.

JIVELEKIAN. I've heard. I'm thinking about it. I don't know what we can do. I would certainly like to finish this game of *scambile*.

FARMER. Our intellectuals, they say, poets, and professors, they are in jail, and some of them have been shot. Shall we raise money?

JIVELEKIAN. Yes, I think raising money would be a very good idea.

FARMER. How much money?

JIVELEKIAN. Well, twenty-eight thousand dollars.

FARMER. What shall we do with money?

JIVELEKIAN. Send it to Armenia, of course.

FARMER. So the Russians will eat it? Oh, no, thank you very much Dr. Jivelekian, we have done foolish things in the past, and we will do foolish things in the future, but we are not going to send our twenty-eight thousand dollars to the Russian invaders.

JIVELEKIAN. Send the money to the Armenians in jail.

FARMER. You must be very innocent of the world, Doctor. The Russians wouldn't let the Armenians in jail have a pomegranate apiece, let alone money.

JIVELEKIAN. Is your back all right?

FARMER. It seems a little improved.

JIVELEKIAN. Go and talk to somebody over there about these matters, and be sure to argue with him.

FARMER. Argue? Why?

JIVELEKIAN. It will make your back feel better. It is amazing how any Armenian feels that he is entitled to intrude on any other Armenian simply because each of them is Armenian.

KNADJIAN. It's not amazing at all. We are a small people, and we have been in geographical, political, cultural, economic, and religious trouble for a long time. We need one another, every last one of us.

JIVELEKIAN. Are you saying I should not have asked the farmer to go away? Is that it, if so I will call the farmer back.

KNADJIAN. No, my friend, I am not saying any such thing, but I am saying that it is perfectly reasonable for any Armenian to make demands on any other Armenian solely because they are Armenians. If we can't bother one another as long as we are on this earth, can we do so in heaven? I am a Presbyterian preacher, and I do not recall that being free to bother another Armenian is one of the promises of the Christian heaven.

JIVELEKIAN. Of course it isn't. Besides, I did suffer the fool—oh, please forgive me, I must not be so crude, so rude, so unkind, the man is not a fool, he is a farmer, but in any case I did suffer him, I listened to him, I gave him the best advice I was able to give, there is no need for every Presbyterian preacher who comes along to nag at me that I am neither a good Armenian nor a good Christian. Now, if the truth is told I am in fact not much of a Christian, I don't really think it is anywhere near as good a religion as one or two of the others, and while I am not prepared to remark that there really is nothing special about being an Armenian, I also cannot say that that fact alone permits any of us to believe we are entitled to anything anybody else is not entitled to.

KNADJIAN. Do you know what you are talking about?

JIVELEKIAN. Of course not. The farmer took my mind from the peace I came here for, and then your Presbyterian reproach annoyed me so deeply, because you know we are friends, that I have forgotten really how to think, so you tell me what are we talking about?

KNADJIAN. He wanted to know what we are to do about the situation in Armenia.

JIVELEKIAN. I see, and what did we tell him. I, as a doctor, and you, as a preacher. What were we able to manage between us as a message of wisdom or comfort for the farmer. Did I say perhaps the most sensible thing for you to do, sir, is to attend to your vineyard, prune your vines, water them, harvest your grapes, eat them, give away some, and the rest sell to the packing houses or the wineries. Did I say that?

KNADJIAN. You did not.

JIVELEKIAN. Should I have said it?

KNADJIAN. Perhaps, if you might manage to say it without being sarcastic.

JIVELEKIAN. I am not sarcastic, I was not sarcastic, I hate sarcasm, I hate sarcastic people, the people of Bitlis are sarcastic people, I hate the people of Bitlis, they are always pointing out the pretenses and pomposities of other people, I am afraid of the people of Bitlis, I know they will see through me and laugh at my silly eccentricities, my little vanities, my pride, or whatever else in me that is flawed and unworthy—the people of Bitlis will see it and say something sarcastic about it. God deliver me from the people of Bitlis.

BITLIS.   Excuse me, I couldn't help overhearing a little of what you
were saying. Do I understand you are looking for somebody from
Bitlis to perhaps give you valuable guidance in a matter of business.
I am from Bitlis.

JIVELEKIAN.   How do you do, how do you do?

BITLIS.   How can I be of help to you, sir.

JIVELEKIAN.   I am a doctor, and I get these pains at the back of my
head.

BITLIS.   Very simple, doctor. When you go home tonight put your
feet in a tub of hot water and at the same time drink four glasses
of hot lemonade. The pain will go.

JIVELEKIAN.   Thank you.

BITLIS.   Don't mention it.

MOUSH.   Why are you sitting here playing cards when Armenia is
bleeding from its terrible wounds?

KNADJIAN.   Well, we are having a short rest before returning to our
sorrow about Armenia. And who are you, sir?

MOUSH.   Surely you can tell from my speech that I am a man from
Moush.

KNADJIAN.   Yes, that's true. And your profession is . . . watchmaking?

MOUSH.   There has never been a watchmaker from Moush.

JIVELEKIAN.   Furthermore, we are not playing cards, although we sat
here in the *expectation* of doing so, but who can play cards when
people from Bitlis and Moush come up and ask questions?

MOUSH.   The interruption of your card game costs you no blood.

JIVELEKIAN.   I thank God for that. Have we your permission to play?

MOUSH.   There is always time to play. You are grown men. This man
is a preacher. A Protestant of course, but still some sort of a Christian
and some sort of an Armenian. I don't know what you are.

JIVELEKIAN.   I am a doctor.

MOUSH.   Of philosophy or something like that?

JIVELEKIAN.   A medical doctor.

MOUSH.   A medical doctor in this place of patriotic idleness, instead
of in his office, healing the sick and comforting the halt?

JIVELEKIAN.   This is in fact my lunch hour. I must also have a moment
of diversion, the same as everybody else.

MOUSH.   I do not have a moment of diversion. I have never had a
moment of diversion. I stand guard over the soul of Armenia at
all times.

JIVELEKIAN. I really would like to play this hand of *scambile* with the good Protestant preacher here.

MOUSH. Which doctor *are* you doctor? By name?

JIVELEKIAN. Jivelekian, from Boston, Harvard Medical School.

MOUSH. I've heard of you.

JIVELEKIAN. And may I ask which man of Moush are you?

MOUSH. I am Baghdasar.

JIVELEKIAN. Baghdasar of Moush, is that right?

MOUSH. That is right.

JIVELEKIAN. Have you a family name?

MOUSH. Der Kaprielian. Baghdasar Der Kaprielian.

JIVELEKIAN. That's very impressive, very impressive indeed. And what is your profession, sir? What do you do for a living?

MOUSH. Well, in season I add corks to wine bottles.

JIVELEKIAN. You add corks to wine bottles.

MOUSH. For Krikor Arakelian.

JIVELEKIAN. How long is the season?

MOUSH. A week. A solid week. The sorrow and darkness. . . . Have you ever put corks into the mouths of wine bottles, Doctor?

JIVELEKIAN. No, I haven't.

MOUSH. Stick to your own work, then. Who will ever know, who will ever guess what I have been through in order to earn the money for bread?

KNADJIAN. You are quite right, no man knows another's suffering.

MOUSH. But a week of corks and bottle-mouths is not the same as being in jail in Armenia.

KNADJIAN. That's quite true, there is a difference.

MOUSH. So what are we going to do about it? Our brothers are in jail.

JIVELEKIAN. We certainly can't do anything from here, so perhaps you will permit us to continue our game, after all.

MOUSH. If you insist on being irresponsible and insensitive, then by all means go ahead, but do not expect me to think of you as an Armenian.

JIVELEKIAN. But I am an Armenian.

MOUSH. Only in word, not in act. God help us one and all if *you* are to be our salvation.

JIVELEKIAN. Ah, well, let me put it this way. I do my best. I do my best.

MOUSH. Your best is not good enough.

JIVELEKIAN.   All right, Reverend Knadjian, what shall we do? Shall we sit here and chat with our countrymen, shall we sit here and play cards, or shall we sit here and sip coffee?

KNADJIAN.   Well, Dr. Jivelekian, I see no reason why we shouldn't do all three. We certainly have *already* done them in any case, haven't we?

JIVELEKIAN.   We have not played cards.

KNADJIAN.   Ah, well, perhaps we can forget cards.

VAN.   I understand you gentlemen have been discussing the realities of very recent Armenian history. What is your position?

JIVELEKIAN.   You take this one, Reverend Knadjian.

VAN.   Oh, you are a man of the church, are you? From your clothes it is not perfectly clear, although your face does have the earnestness of a man who believes in prayer. Can praying help recent Armenian history, Reverend?

KNADJIAN.   Yes, I think we are all pretty much in agreement about that, since we are Christian, but I would say that praying must be supplemented by goods and action.

VAN.   I see. Goods and action. What goods? What action?

KNADJIAN.   Well, first of course we pray, and then we consider what our countrymen need—money, medicine, food, clothing, shelter, but most of all the moral support of a powerful nation which can force the oppressor to cease and desist, and to leave our country and return to his own.

VAN.   And who would that nation be, may I ask?

KNADJIAN.   Well, our neighbors are the Persians, the Syrians, the Turks, the Greeks, and the Russians. But of course the Russians have invaded our country, and they are the biggest and most powerful of our neighbors. Of the others none is powerful enough to force the Russians away, and so we must think of a powerful nation which is not a neighbor.

VAN.   England?

KNADJIAN.   England could do the job if England would be willing to do it.

VAN.   Italy?

KNADJIAN.   No, Italy is not powerful enough. And for that matter neither is France. The truth is only England in Europe can do it, and in the rest of the world only America can do it.

VAN.   Then, we must ask America to help us.

KNADJIAN.   We have done so—officially, and with proper intelligence, but America has refused.

VAN.   So now what do we do?

KNADJIAN.   Well, unless we are willing to believe that perhaps the Russians will *not* be oppressors of our people, we must think about trying to drive the Russians out of Armenia. And that means that we must raise money and buy goods and pay to ship them to Armenia, and we must hire experts of all kinds, and pay them to do their work.

VAN.   We don't have money like that.

KNADJIAN.   Yes, the problem is a difficult and complicated one.

VAN.   Well, now, about these Russians in Armenia, what are they doing?

KNADJIAN.   Their propaganda claims that they are rescuing Armenia from its enemies, within and without, and they are bringing hospitals, schools, industry, agriculture, security and peace to the Armenian people.

VAN.   Do you believe that?

KNADJIAN.   I suppose not, but at the same time if we can't throw the Russians out, we are almost *obliged* to believe it, aren't we, or at any rate to believe some of it. We don't have any choice. We have fought many losing battles. We really ought not to fight any more.

VAN.   I don't know, I don't know. I am from Van, and we have lost so many souls.

KNADJIAN.   Yes, we are all in sorrow.

BITLIS.   What is it now, you two? Have you made another man unhappy?

JIVELEKIAN.   I don't think so, but if we have, it has not been intentional.

BITLIS.   It doesn't matter about that part of it, you shouldn't say things to good Armenians and make them unhappy. That man over there from Moush, he is in tears.

JIVELEKIAN.   What is he in tears *about*?

BITLIS.   Armenia, of course. When, when, when is Armenia going to be permitted to be free?

KNADJIAN.   Well, we are all concerned about that. We are all asking God that question.

BITLIS.   Since God has not answered the question, let us ask somebody else.

MOUSH.   What is your suggestion? Who shall we ask?

BITLIS. Woodrow Wilson.

KNADJIAN. Well, of course we might ask our friend Woodrow Wilson, but I am afraid he is dead.

MOUSH. Woodrow Wilson is dead? Are you sure?

KNADJIAN. Yes, he died quite sometime ago. Of a broken heart, they say.

JIVELEKIAN. As well as a good variety of other things. The fact is he had a stroke.

BITLIS. Heartbreak, heartbreak killed our only friend in the world, the father of Armenia Restored, Mr. Woodrow Wilson. Oh, this is a sad day.

MOUSH. Doom, doom, doom. Is that to be forever the lot of Armenians?

VAN. Never. Don't say that. We have been stopped here and there and now and then, but in the end let us not forget that we have always moved on. Shame on you men of Moush and Bitlis, giving up to despair. We of Van believe in Armenia, we believe in Armenians.

MOUSH. Do you believe in Russians? They have occupied our country.

VAN. Yes, I believe in Russians.

MOUSH. Do not say that, sir. You will force me to the knife.

VAN. Look here, if it's Russians who have taken the chair of government in Armenia, hadn't we better watch and wait before we begin to stick knives into one another. Where all this is happening is very far from here. I understand it is eight thousand miles from the Patriotic Club on Ventura Avenue in Fresno, California to the seat of government in Erevan, Armenia.

MOUSH. Nine thousand, and the Russians are sitting in that seat. I want them out.

VAN. Drop them a line, tell them you can't sleep for the sorrow in your heart, or tell them that if they don't get out, you will write a second letter.

MOUSH. It is stupid to argue with a man from Van. Let me say to my neighbor from Bitlis, we must not let our beloved cities fall away from Armenia.

JIVELEKIAN. They have already fallen away, they are not even a part of that Armenia which is now governed by the Russians. Bitlis and Moush are part of Turkey, gentlemen.

MOUSH. I beg of you, don't say that.

JIVELEKIAN. I'm sorry, it's true.

MOUSH. How did it, how did it *ever*, please tell me sir how did it happen, how did it happen?

JIVELEKIAN. Woodrow Wilson drew a map of the true and real Armenia, but neither he nor anybody else saw to it that the Armenians became the lords of their own country, and the map grew smaller and smaller until it was almost nothing but Erevan and two or three vineyards around it—not even as much land as we have in Fresno *county*.

MOUSH. Is this true?

JIVELEKIAN. Yes, it is, I am sorry, yes, it is.

MOUSH. *Vy*, alas, glorious Armenia, alas majestic Moush, gone, gone, torn away from one another. I refuse to speak.

JIVELEKIAN. This is a place of rest, why is everybody here so restless?

BITLIS. Perhaps you will answer your own question, but if you can't do that, isn't it becauses we are all of us here in mourning for Mother Armenia? Isn't it because we are at the funeral of our beloved nation?

KNADJIAN. Yes, we are all very much concerned about the second invasion of the Russians.

MOUSH. We drove them out the first time, and it did seem that now at last we would be a free and independent nation, but no, the Russians came back, and they are now sitting in Erevan. Why? Why does God give us so little reason to thank Him? You are a man of the church, although a Protestant, tell us why?

KNADJIAN. Well, of course I am not any more pleased about the unhappy situation in Armenia than you are. We are all of us very unhappy about having the invaders back a second time, but I wonder if we have a right to take the attitude that it is God who has brought them back a second time.

BITLIS. Did God bring them in the first time?

KNADJIAN. Well, I'm not sure we can believe *that*, either.

JIVELEKIAN. If we are going to drag God into this, hadn't we better begin at the beginning? Did God create the earth, or did the earth happen as the consequence of some other order of event, entirely? That is, not a creation, at all.

BITLIS. How can that be? What are you saying?

KNADJIAN. Yes, even these unschooled men are astonished at such talk. It is heresy.

JIVELEKIAN.   It is meant to be *only* science. If you are going to forget your schooling, I am not going to forget mine, these good men deserve the latest information that is available to the human race.

MOUSH.   What are you talking about? Are you being professors with peasants, is that it? Talk our language.

JIVELEKIAN.   I am asking how can we blame God for bringing the Russians to Armenia the first time and then the second time, when first of all we are not sure God did any such thing, and in the second place we don't even know if God brought the human race itself to the earth—in the first place.

MOUSH.   Of course God did it. God did it all, and that's the end of the matter, it's what we believe, and we don't have any reason, therefore, not to believe it.

JIVELEKIAN.   Well, there is *that*, of course, but it isn't scientific.

BITLIS.   What is scientific, if you don't mind? Perhaps it will help us to understand why God has betrayed us twice—recently. A thousand times, twice, in times gone by. And we are Christians. So what is scientific?

JIVELEKIAN.   I can't speak for all who respect science, but I think I may say that science is simply the study of the truth about everything. You find out in science, whereas in religion you believe, you agree to believe, and you pay no attention to new discoveries in the realm of truth.

BITLIS.   Are you saying that what we believe, what we have believed for so long is untrue? Are you an Armenian, or something else?

KNADJIAN.   Let me intercede here for the Doctor. He is indeed a Christian, a good man, a believer in God, a lover of humanity, and a true Armenian, but he is also a doctor of medicine, he saves human lives by medicine and surgery, and he knows that if he had not learned medicine, he would not have been able to save lives.

MOUSH.   Let him save the life of Armenia—if he knows so much.

JIVELEKIAN.   I will certainly do my best to help save the life of Armenia, just as you will do your best, as each of us will. That is both science and religion—and perhaps even art.

MOUSH.   I don't understand.

KNADJIAN.   Gentlemen, boys, men of Van, Moush, and Bitlis, patriotic Armenians one and all, let me suggest that we bear in mind that we are at a disadvantage at this moment insofar as speaking intelligently with one another is concerned, for we are unhappy about our beloved Armenia. In other words, let us make a point of not fighting one another.

BITLIS. Who's fighting? Our brothers in Armenia have been fighting, and many of them have been killed and injured, while we have been living like kings in Fresno, California.

MOUSH. We have been living, but not like kings. A man dying in Armenia is living like a king. A man living like a king in Fresno is actually dying like a dog. Is this a life? Is this living?

VAN. Well, we are here, in any case, and we were not forced to come here. Of course this is a life, it is a good life. Of course this is living.

MOUSH. This is dying, this is not living at all. Our brothers are living, even the ones who are dead. And I'll tell you why, too. They are home, they are in Armenia, they are in the land under the sun of our noble race, but where are we—we are somewhere else, far away.

JIVELEKIAN. I would like to suggest that it is a very good thing that we are in fact here. This is a great place to be.

MOUSH. How can you say that. Is Fresno Moush? It is not. Is it Bitlis? It is not. Is it Van? It is not.

JIVELEKIAN. Of course not. It is Fresno, though. It is where so many of us have made ourselves at home, doing our work as we know how to do it, buying and cultivating vineyards, learning and practicing professions, opening stores, practicing crafts. Gentlemen, we are here. We are not in Armenia.

VAN. Please don't remind me of that.

JIVELEKIAN. Don't you like it here?

VAN. It is not what I expected.

JIVELEKIAN. Well, we are all of us always disappointed when we go to a place about which we have heard many many beautiful stories. What did you expect?

VAN. I expected a much better life than this life.

JIVELEKIAN. Well, that may be a personal matter. Perhaps you must think about it a little longer. You look very well for a man of fifty or more. You wear good clothes. What is it that you don't like?

VAN. The water. It's not as good as the water of Van. The greens are not as green, either. Parsley, onions, bell peppers, cucumbers, they are all greener and better in Van.

JIVELEKIAN.   Those are serious failings, no doubt about it, but I find it hard to believe that you do not like the water of Fresno. It is the best water I have ever drunk.

VAN.   You have never quenched your thirst on the water of Van?

JIVELEKIAN.   Alas, no.

VAN.   The water of Van is water. This is also water, but it is not the water of Van, it does not give life to the soul, it gives life only to the body. Armenians are people with soul. And the soul must have air, light, and water.

JIVELEKIAN.   It seems to me that we are forgetting to be grateful, which is a very foolish thing. Gentlemen, we are lucky, we are very lucky to be in Fresno, to have our families here, and it is wrong not to remember this.

BITLIS.   I remember it. I am very happy to be here, but that doesn't mean I don't also remember Bitlis—we were up, up, high up, far, far below we saw the river of Bitlis racing through the deep valley to the heart of Bitlis itself. I can't forget that, can I, just because we are here?

JIVELEKIAN.   No, that's quite true, but you are here, so enjoy it.

MOUSH.   Do we have to?

KNADJIAN.   Ah, here, you, are, sir. Please sit down. Take my chair. I'll get another.

PAPAZIAN.   No, no, I shall stay only a moment, I simply must go to a doctor about my ankles. I only want to say, countrymen, each of you, let us thank God that Armenia is still there, and that we are still here, and that we owe it all to the grace and goodness of God.

MOUSH.   What did he say, this Protestant? Countrymen, something and something.

VAN.   Be careful, this is Reverend Papazian. He has given sermons in American churches in the English language.

MOUSH.   I know who he is. He thinks the Americans are the real people, and he tries to be like them, and to think like them, because he thinks Armenians are too backward and too loud and too unreasonable and too angry about everything, and of course he means me, he means you, and he means that man from Bitlis, he doesn't mean himself when he thinks about Armenians, he means us, he thinks Armenia would be just fine if *we* had been killed instead of the people who were killed, but we *were* killed because we are the same kind as the people who were killed, and that's why we are always thrashing around from the pains we knew before we died, and that's why we always want to know before we die that our dying helped, that our terrible dying helped Armenia remain Armenia, what does a pompous little Protestant preacher know about Armenia, and Armenians, this little black-bearded man is no Armenian, he is not American, he is a member of no nationality because he thinks he and God are comrades who go about spreading benedictions everywhere. Well, sir, little sire, just forget the bargain sanctity and spread some guns and bread to Armenians, that's all.

PAPAZIAN.   The man is obviously insane, but I forgive him.

MOUSH.   Yes, well, I don't forgive you. Who asked you to come here and insult the tragic Armenian soul?

KNADJIAN.   That's enough, sir, that's enough, whatever it is that moves you to anger and sorrow, do not take it out on a perfectly innocent preacher of the gospel. He is a good man, he works hard, he helps everybody he can, please do not imagine you must believe he is your enemy. You Van, you Bitlis, please take your friend away. Get him a small coffee, sit down together, think, think before you speak, think twice before you shout, think three times before you go mad. Tell the waiter to bring the bill to me, I'll pay for it.

BITLIS.   Oh, you are most generous, sir. Three coffees, five cents each, fifteen cents. You have just saved Armenia, no doubt about it. How can we ever thank you? Shall we build a monument to you, and to your little black-bearded brother, and put it in the Court House Park of Fresno? Why do Protestant preachers feel that the people are all fools?

JIVELEKIAN.   Gentlemen, gentlemen, I can only speak for myself, a practicing physician and surgeon, and I must say that my heart is sick with sorrow, not only because of recent developments in Armenia, of the second return of the Russians to the seat of government, but because of recent developments right here, among us. Can't we understand that this sort of annoyance and belittlement of one another is terribly destructive, that it will soon enough destroy us? That we will become a people without a culture, and must therefore perish forever?

MOUSH.   We shall *not* perish. Armenia shall not perish. Armenians shall not perish. Doctors and preachers may perish, and let them perish, that is no affair of ours, but we shall not, we shall never agree to perish, the more appealing the world makes perishing the more we shall refuse to perish. We are Armenians, and even though we are eight or nine thousand miles away from where we were born, we are still in Armenia, we are still there, and this very place, this patriotic coffee house, is Armenia. Preachers and doctors can go to hell. The people lie in their Armenian graves, or stand in their homes, or sit and stand in this place, and refuse to be polite about indestructible Armenia.

KNADJIAN. Dr. Jivelekian I'm afraid it is useless to remain in this unhappy atmosphere, and so let me put down these cards and say goodbye, I must go.

JIVELEKIAN. But the game hasn't even *started*, Reverend Knadjian. Surely you don't expect me to waste the opportunity to test your mettle at cards. I've paid the dime for the deck of cards, for one hour. I shuffled, you cut, I dealt, and now suddenly you stand and say you must leave this unhappy atmosphere, you must go. What about my dime?

KNADJIAN. I love the game, and I would gladly test your mettle in the playing of the game, but we sat down at a time of great unhappiness in the people who come here every day. And of course when they see a man of the Church with a man of Medicine, it is understandable that they want to talk, but when they do talk, they argue, they ask impossible questions, it wears out a man's soul just trying to know what they mean. Sir, if you don't mind what do you mean?

MOUSH. I mean exactly what I said, exactly what I have always said, exactly what every Armenian with any salt and vinegar in his veins would say. We are here. We are Armenians. Whether we are from Van, Moush, Bitlis, Harpoot, Dikranagert, Trabizond, Erzeroum, Malatia, or wherever, we are here, and we are Armenians. And Van is there, and Moush is there, and Bitlis is there, and all of the other Armenian cities are there, and our dead are there, and perhaps a few of our living are still there, God help them one and all, surrounded by enemies and danger, famine and homelessness, but let us just remember this, that whoever they are which are still there, in the cities of the real Armenia, not the Russian Armenia, *they* are the nation, and the nation shall not end, it is the will of God, it is the will of the World, it is the will of History and Truth, it is the will of Art that Armenia shall not end, Armenia shall endure, that is what I mean, sir, that is exactly what I mean, what do *you* mean?

BITLIS. I am dumbfounded. Where the devil did you ever learn to talk that way? Was that *you*?

MOUSH. It *was* me. It is me. But it is really Armenia, it is Moush, it is Shah-Mouradian, the singer of the song of our country.

KNADJIAN. I knew him. I admired him. I was his friend.

JIVELEKIAN. All the more reason to sit down and pick up your cards and start the game.

KNADJIAN. At a time like this? How can you be so insensitive. This good man has been talking with the soul and voice of Armenia itself, and all you want is for me to sit down and play cards? Doctor, are you sure you aren't sick yourself?

JIVELEKIAN. No, no, I'm in perfect health.

KNADJIAN. Then, please be good enough to be moved by this good man and the amazing voice with which he says the amazing words of truth about Armenia.

JIVELEKIAN. I was moved by the words, I am moved by the voice, do you think I am less an Armenian than yourself, or less than anybody else, anywhere? But there comes a time when even the most profoundly passionate Armenian wants to forget it for a moment and play a game of cards. That moment has come. Sit down, pick up your cards, let the game start. Am I right?

MOUSH. Yes, I think a pleasant game of cards is sometimes a good thing.

JIVELEKIAN. There. He said so himself. The very man who said Armenia, Armenia.

KNADJIAN. Well, as long as you've paid the dime, very well, but remember I do not really believe in cards.

JIVELEKIAN. That's all right. A lot of people who go to church don't really believe in Jesus, either.

KNADJIAN. A lot of people who go to hell don't believe in heaven either.

MOUSH. No, no, don't play the ace, play the eight. Have you no sense at all of the appropriate?

HARPOOT. I am from Harpoot. There are more people from Harpoot in Fresno than from any other city in Armenia. I could not help noticing the commotion around this card table from far across this smoke-filled room, and of course many of the words that were spoken here carried across the room, so that I know you have been talking about matters of great concern. Well, I stood there and watched and listened, and suddenly it seemed to me I had better come here and protest. Let us be practical, gentlemen. Let us be reasonable. Let us be men of the world. Do you think you can talk about Armenia and leave out Harpoot? It is impossible. But you have talked and you have talked but not once has anybody mentioned Harpoot. What are we, orphans or something?

MOUSH.   What do you want, a medal?

HARPOOT.   Never mind a sarcastic medal, all I want is a straight answer to a simple question. Is Harpoot a part of the sorrow of Armenia, or not?

BITLIS.   Why should you ask that question? What is the real purpose in asking such a question? Why do you wish to ridicule us?

HARPOOT.   Me? Ridicule? I'm scared to death, almost, to open my mouth, for fear one or another of you, from Van, Moush, or Bitlis, will tell me to go back to my stupid rug business. Well, it is true that I am in the rug business, and that many of the people of Harpoot are in the rug business, it is an honorable business, and there is great beauty and art in many of the rugs that are in my shop.

VAN.   Ah, please, please, sir, whoever you are, hasn't the Armenian name suffered enough because of the rug sellers? Why did you even mention that you sell rugs? Can you expect us to be sympathetic with a man whose sole purpose in life is to make a big fat profit from some perfectly ignorant and unsuspecting American who wants to believe he has become successful and prosperous. I hate rug sellers. I have always hated them.

HARPOOT.   There, you see, everybody hates me. What right have you got to hate me for trying to make a living and to live in a nice home and to send my children to college? The rug merchant is a man of importance in all of the great cities of the world.

MOUSH.   Perhaps he is, but it is not quite clear whether he belongs to the Armenian nation or to the Money nation.

HARPOOT.   *What* nation? Money, did you say? What nation is the Money nation? Why are you ganging up on a man from Harpoot? I came here to let you know that my sorrow about the return of the Russians to Armenia is as great as your sorrow. The people of Harpoot will not be outdone in a matter of sorrow. Why are you trying to belittle a man from Harpoot?

VASKEN.   Harpoot? I'm from Harpoot? What's wrong with Harpoot?

HARPOOT.   These men of Van, Moush, Bitlis, and these professional men of Fresno seem to think that the people of Harpoot don't count when it comes to sorrow for Armenia, and they also seem to think that if a man sells rugs he cannot be considered an Armenian, even, he is a member of another nationality, the Money nationality, and I consider that a terrible slander.

VASKEN.   Who's a rug merchant?

HARPOOT.   It happens, countryman, that I am. Here's my card. Giragos Arpiar Der Havasarian at your service. Oriental Rugs. 2228 Mariposa Street. Rare rugs for sale. Also cleaning and repairing.

VASKEN.   I see. I've passed your store many times. You do indeed have good merchandise. Have you ever sold a rug to an Armenian?

HARPOOT.   Only to members of my family. The others of course avoid my place. When will the Armenians learn to buy from Armenian merchants.

BITLIS.   Just as soon as Armenian merchants stop cheating, that's when.

HARPOOT.   Look who's talking. A man from Bitlis. Well, you must surely know from personal experience what you are talking about.

KNADJIAN.   Gentlemen, let us try to speak to one another with respect and a certain amount of charity, in the name of our Lord Christ Jesus.

MOUSH.   You keep Him out of this. He's done enough damage to the Armenian nation. Keep Him in the backroom at the Red Brick Church, and let Him out only on big holy days.

ERZEROUM.   In a family there are many children. Each child has a character of his own. One may be swift in nature, another may be slow. A third may be melancholic, a fourth may be entirely blithe. And so on and so forth. It would be foolish if we imagined that in our family all of the children are alike. Let us not be surprised by any of our children. There is nothing wrong in a man who sells rugs for a living.

KNADJIAN.   Yes, that was nicely put. Are you perhaps a Presbyterian preacher?

ERZEROUM.   No, but I don't consider it a poor profession. I am a farmer.

JIVELEKIAN.   You don't speak like a farmer.

ERZEROUM.   Nobody speaks like a farmer or a rug merchant or anything else of that kind. Every man is who he is before he is what he does for a living. I have watched this corner of this room for a good hour or more and it seems to me that somebody must soon inform us that we do not have to be the only nation in the world, the only nation of all time, which is composed solely of saints, heroes, giants of soul and intellect, marvels of productivity, paragons of virtue. Gentlemen, we belong to the human race, the same as everybody else.

MOUSH.   Of course we belong to the human race, but let us please remember that we belong to the Armenian branch of it, and some of us to the Moush branch of the Armenian branch of it, and these things make a difference.

ERZEROUM.   A small difference, that's true, but only a small difference.

BITLIS.   All well and good, but the cause of our sorrow is Armenia itself, where Armenia is, so it is not necessary to notice that we are a nation of many kinds of people with many kinds of character. I have certainly seen Armenians who might be the descendants of soldiers invading our country from Manchuria, Siberia, Mongolia, China—we do not know about such things. Blue eyes and red hair I have also seen—from invaders who came from England, France, Germany, Sweden. What do we know. We are Armenians. We are from Bitlis or from Van or Moush or somewhere else. Our sorrow is the consequence of a fear that perhaps now after all this time, after centuries, Armenia may be coming to an end—the Russians in the seat of Government in Armenia where Armenia is, and the rest of us faraway learning new languages and living among new peoples and forgetting how to read and write our own language, changing our names, marrying outsiders, letting it go, letting it all go. That is what is making it sorrowful.

VAN.   I am from Van, my wife is from Van, my children although born here are children of Van, we shall never stop being children of Van, and Armenians.

JIVELEKIAN.   I wonder—please do not take this emotionally—I wonder if it is possible for even a man like yourself to remain in Armenia while he and his family live in another place, in America, in California, in Fresno, in the Armenian Quarter of Fresno, is it possible, is it actually possible that he can in fact go on as if he were still in the family home in Van, in Armenia?

VAN. I say it is possible. Furthermore, I say it is necessary. Unless we are to vanish from the face of the earth, swallowed up by the rest of the human race, it is necessary.

MOUSH. My children not only speak Armenian, they go to Armenian school at the Red Brick Church, they read Armenian, they sing classical Armenian in the choir at the church every Sunday and every Holy Day. We are Armenians and we shall continue to be Armenians as long as. . .as long as. . .as long as what shall I say? As long as we. . .what is the word I want?

ERZEROUM. There is no word. We are Armenians while we are Armenians. After that we are not Armenians. But do not despair, there is no way for any of us not to be members of the human race, and in the end isn't that what we are really concerned about? Each of us to be his own special kind of member of the human race? Aren't all of the nations of the world made up of Armenians, as a matter of fact? And are not Armenians made up of all of the other nationalities? We are sorry not for Armenia but for the human race.

DIKRANAGERT. Look here, Armenians. We do not need to use up all of our time and energy feeling sorry about Armenia. There is such a thing as feeling sorry and then feeling something else, and a little later feeling something else, and after a little while feeling something else, and little by little feeling almost hopeful, almost happy. It is possible, Armenians, and it might just be sensible. What do you say we stop feeling sorry? Look, we are here, we are none of us wounded, we are all of us quite healthy, let us enjoy our good fortune.

MOUSH. What about our brothers in Armenia? What shall they enjoy?

DIKRANAGERT. They will enjoy whatever they can, of course. Perhaps they will enjoy nothing more than another morning. What did we enjoy when each of us was in trouble, as of course each of us has been, as we would have had to be even had we not been Armenians, had we been in fact anybody else, anybody at all, fortunate or unfortunate, trouble is the lot of the human race, not the Armenian nation—although lately we have had a good deal more than our share—but what's the good of thinking only of that? Why not move along to a fresh start, a new attitude, a useful program?

VAN. And just who are you, sir?

DIKRANAGERT.   Nobody, nobody, of course. But it is not wise for grown men to let themselves sink into deep and useless melancholy. Can we help our brothers in Armenia? Apparently we can't. Well then hadn't we better see about helping ourselves and one another and our children, and our friends, and our neighbors, and if it comes to that our enemies, why shouldn't we help even our worst enemies, wouldn't that surprise them and make them think about the whole foolishness of hating somebody or being afraid of somebody? I mean, I am from Dikranagert, but I have been gone from there many years, and my six children were all born here, and we are all of us very fortunate and in good health, is it not permissible for us to be grateful for our good luck, and to be no longer in mourning for our brothers in Armenia? We have all of us lost members of the immediate family, but mourning them forever isn't at all sensible, it does nobody any good at all, and it does make us look just a little silly. We have got to stop being in mourning somewhere, sometime. Isn't this the proper place and the proper time?

BITLIS.   We can of course stop mourning and we can of course be grateful for our good luck, but we can't forget, that's all. We just can't forget. A man's father dies, a man doesn't forget his father, ever. He remembers him, he remembers all that he knows about his father, he remembers for the rest of his life. A man's brother disappears, a man can't stop wanting to know what happened to his brother. He can't stop thinking about his brother. Of course it is unwise to mourn the dead forever. The living have a right to our deepest concern, but there is always something of the soul left over for the dead.

KNADJIAN.   Gentlemen, may I volunteer this small thought? At the very least let us just agree among ourselves far from Armenia that we have not forgotten, we will not forget, we shall always remember our family, dead and alive, and in the meantime we shall see to it that we ourselves, each of us, works and lives a decent life, and takes care of his people and is kindly towards all others, and then— yes, I agree with the man from Dikranagert, and then, each of us laughs and sings and in this manner worships God and the Great Mysteries.

JIVELEKIAN.   I had hoped to play out a hand of cards, but it seems to me that the fates will not permit it. Well, then, let me say this to you good Armenians: countrymen, I am a doctor, my office is in the Rowell Building, my name, Arshak Jivelekian is in the phone book, if you take sick, or if a member of your family takes sick, telephone me from the store or wherever you phone from, and I will come to your house and do my best to relieve your pain and restore your health.

MOUSH. Again we have failed. We cannot even talk together about the same thing. Our minds wander. Well, all the same, I say long live Armenia.

KASPARIAN. What's going on, gentlemen? A messenger came running to tell me there is a crisis here? What crisis is it?

PAPAZIAN. I have been sitting here and listening and all I can say is that there is indeed a crisis here. We cannot speak to one another in a meaningful way, every one of us is a leader, a general of the army, a king, a president, the greatest thinker of all time, and so on and so forth. This is the curse of the Armenian race. We are a nation of great men. We do not have a population. We do not have people. I have sat here in absolute sorrow, disbelief, despair, pain, and a kind of strange pride—thank God we are who we are and what we are. After all, there has got to be a reason why we are all equally great. We are finished, I suppose, but who knows, who knows, perhaps all of the others are finished, and *we* are not.

MOUSH. Who asked you? What right have you got to give a Protestant sermon here in the Patriotic Club? I've seen you, I've seen you, I know who you are, and there is one thing I can tell you. You want to be an American, that's all. So be an American. But don't tell me all about myself and all about my family and all about my heart and mind.

PAPAZIAN. I said nice things. I certainly tried to say nice things.

MOUSH. Keep your nice things to yourself, please. You are nobody, you said so yourself, while the rest of us are national heroes.

VAN. It is not necessary to be rude at a time like this. Let us at least permit these three men of the church to speak to one another in peace.

BITLIS. Peace? But there is no peace. The Russians sit in the chair of government in Armenia. Is that peace? If this is the end, we have the right to know it, and to gather ourselves together in dispersion, in memory of what we were and what we had and what is now forever lost. Excuse me, Father, but I went to the school of the missionaries in Bitlis—it was the only way any of us there could get a little education.

KASPARIAN. It is desirable to acquire knowledge. The missionaries did not convert anybody to Christianity, they only took some of the Christians away from the national church and put them into their church.

VAN. The international church, perhaps? Isn't it the aspiration of all civilized people to become citizens of the world rather than merely citizens of one country? I must confess that I am strongly tempted to aspire, now, to such citizenship. Now, that it does appear as if our long day is coming to a close.

KASPARIAN. Yes, we may find that Armenia will soon be a memory for most of us, and that we shall be happy to share the life and culture of the place and people where we now live, but I do not believe any of us, believers or unbelievers, can give up hope, short of the grave. I do not believe anyone here is prepared to really believe that Armenia is finished. Let every Armenian in the world be a leader who leads nobody anywhere. Let the land of Armenia be divided among its neighbors. Let foreigners sit in the chair of government. Still, I do not believe any of us is willing or able to believe that Armenia is finished, that it is a thing of the past.

DIKRANAGERT. Is it necessary for Armenia to be Armenia now and forever?

KASPARIAN. No, of course not. But it is also not necessary for the human race to be the human race now and forever. We know nothing. We do nothing. It is all known and done without our knowledge or participation. I must return to my small daily chores. Will you let me help you to the street?

PAPAZIAN. Yes, yes, by all means, let us all return to our small daily chores. I am ashamed of my foolish disability at a time when I should be vigorous and swift.

KNADJIAN. I must go, also. Goodbye, gentlemen. Have faith, have conversations, have arguments, have fun, this may be a better beginning than we know, and a better ending than any ending heretofore.

MOUSH. Heretofore? Ah, well, I did not go to the missionary schools.

BITLIS. Long live the human spirit!

VAN. Long live the Armenian spirit!

GILIGIA. Just a minute. Let me put in my two cents worth. I am from Giligia.

BITLIS

A Play in One Act

A topographic map of Bitlis in the late nineteenth century showing the main river (Bitlis Chai) and the quarter of the Saroyan family, Tsapergor (Sapkor Mahallasi) and its riverlet (Sapkor Su). (Photo after Lynch, *Armenian Travels and Studies*, 1901, vol. II, between pp. 146-7) Below, a view of Bitlis with its fortress taken at the turn of the century. (Photo courtesy of Sarah Bedrosian)

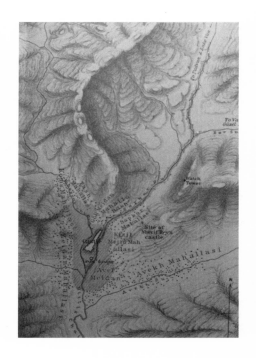

Bitlis today: above, during Saroyan's visit in 1964 (photo Bedros Zobian); below, a view of the fortress in the 1970s (photo Centre de Documentation Arménien, Paris).

At Van on the way to Bitlis, Saroyan is accompanied by a Turkish officer, Bedros Zobian to the left, and Ara Altounian on the right. Below, on the road ten kilometers from Bitlis, Saroyan is seen with the 1958 Chevrolet of Ara Altounian used during the trip. (Photos courtesy of Bedros Zobian)

Above, lunch time on the way from Bitlis to Diyarbekir, May 18, 1964. From left to right: the Turkish journalist Fikret Otyam with the main characters of the play *Bitlis*—Ara, Bedros and Bill. Center, Bedros Zobian and his wife Seta visiting Saroyan in Fresno, three years later in May 1967. (Photos courtesy of Bedros Zobian) Below, a Saroyan book-drawing entitled "[Lord] Byron the Friend of Armenia," executed by Saroyan on March 19, 1975, four days before he started writing the play *Bitlis*. (Saroyan Archive CSUF, photo Dickran Kouymjian)

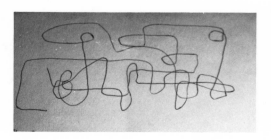

Saroyan in the midst of a welcoming party in Bitlis clutching a bouquet of wild flowers gathered from the surrounding mountains. Below, Saroyan and Bedros Zobian on a street in Bitlis, May 17, 1964. (Photos courtesy of Bedros Zobian)

Saroyan sitting on the very spot in Bitlis where his family's ancestral houses were once located. Below, he is seen standing next to the hearth, the only vestige, of the house of his maternal grandmother's family, the Garoghlanians, Bitlis, May 17, 1964. (Photos courtesy of Bedros Zobian)

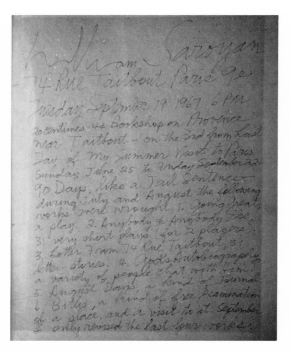

A long inscription and drawing by William Saroyan inside the cover of a book purchased in Paris on the same day, September 19, 1967. Six new works of July and August of that year are listed including the sixth entitled "Bitlis, a kind of free examination of a place, and a visit to it." This is not the play but probably a version of a longer prose work. The drawing is on the backside of the front cover; the text faces it. (Saroyan Archive, CSUF, photos Dickran Kouymjian)

Saroyan Taitbout Paris Sunday March 23 1975 10:35 A.M.   Bitlis

Ara: Well, this is Bitlis, the home of your people, what do you
think of it?
Bill: This is a little Turkish restaurant on the main street of
Bitlis where we are to have tea and bread and cheese. Even so, it is
almost unbelievable that I am here, I am in Bitlis, that my family has
lived here for centuries.
Bedros: Well, they certainly welcomed us, they certainly welcomed
you---the Mayor, school teachers, business men, and at least five hundred
people. What did you think when you saw them?
Bill: I thought well it's damned nice of the Mayor and all the
others of course, and it was pleasant to see their good faces and to
hear their good voices, but let's not imagine that I don't know somebody
has instructed them to do this.
Ara: Of course, of course, people don't do things of this kind without
authorization, without permission, or without instructions. The Turks
in Istanbul and Ankara want to welcome a son of Bitlis on a visit to
his ancestral home, even if he is a gaouir, an infidel, and an Armenia.
They think of you as one of themselves, a son of Anadole, as they put it.
Nobody says Turkish or Armenian. It wouldn't be polite. But here's
Ahkhmed with tea and so let us refresh ourselves.
Ahkhmed: Tell him, tell him, please, he even looks to be one of us.
Bedros: He's saying in Turkish tell him he looks to be one of us.
Bill: Yes, and I must say that all of the young men seemed to be
members of my own family, cousins, as I said to the Mayor, and to a few
of the boys.
Ara: Well, the Kourd is like the Armenian, he is like us. Take a
sip of this aromatic tea, stir in the sugar, lots of sugar, it will refresh
your soul. And of course although it is officially frowned upon to remark
that you are a Kourd, almost everybody in Bitlis is a Kourd. There was
not one Armenian in the crowd. I can spot one in a flash. Not one, not
one, and Bitlis for centuries, calledBaghesh was one of the main cities
of Armenia.
Bill: It still is, as far as I am concerned. Yes, the tea is
refreshing. My grandmother Lucintak Saraoghlanian made tea like this.
In our house on San Benito Avenue in Fresno we drank tea all day in
the winter.
Ara: And in the summer?
Bill: We ate watermelon. Well, at any rate, I did, for I do love
and need lots of water. Ahkhmed seems like a decent sort, is he a Turk?
Is he a mixture? He looks like one of us.
Bedros: We all of us share the same earth and have for a long time,
and so we are bound to look like one another, but Ahkhmed is a Turk.
Bill: Not a Kourd, he certainly doesn't look like the boys in the
crowd that met is at the Gate to the Castle. And what is the Castle?
Ara: Ahkhmed is not a Kourd, he is a member of the minority in
Bitlis, a Turk, but he is the owner of a restaurant, and that makes
the difference. He serves food and drink to customers, and he wants
customers, and so in a sense he is not really very much of anything,
he belongs to the nationality of cooks and waiters.
Bill: Seems like a nice guy.
Ara: In a nice time anybody is a nice time. Who should know that
better than yourself. An American. A writer. A student of the human
character. Ahkhmed will be delighted to have the small sum he charges
for his good food, which I will double so that when we come again he
will remember us, and of course we shall come this afternoon, for this
is the only restaurant in town---well, the only one for travelers.
Bill: Why will you double the sum? Ara, you must understand this is
not simple curiosity, I suspect there is something formal in that, a kind
of statement to him and to those he talks to that you want known. Am I
entirely mistaken or is there something to this. A kind of Bitlis or
Kourdish or Turkish or regional tradition?
Ara: Yes, precisely---first his bill will be quite small, not quite
enough, second I may double it without offending him, I can't triple it for
that would be charity, and he has pride---he will say we are people of
sense and courtesy. It is important, even for only one day. 11:05 A

The first page of Saroyan's typescript of *Bitlis* written in Paris, March 23, 1975.
The illustration is after the photocopy given to Dickran Kouymjian by the author.
The original typescript is in the William Saroyan Archive, Bancroft Library, University
of California, Berkeley.

THE PEOPLE

ARA, *Armenian traveling companion from Istanbul*
BILL SAROYAN, *Armenian-American writer*
BEDROS, *editor of* Marmara, *Armenian daily newspaper of Istanbul*
AKHMED, *Turkish restaurant owner in Bitlis*

THE PLACE

Bitlis, the ancestral hometown of the Saroyan family, part of historic Armenia, now in Turkey.

THE TIME

Sunday, May 19, 1964.

NOTE. The play was written in one act with seven scenes in Paris between March 23 and 29, 1975. The scenes have been omitted by the editor.

ARA.   Well, this is Bitlis, the home of your people. What do you think of it?

BILL.   This is a little Turkish restaurant on the main street of Bitlis where we are to have tea and bread and cheese. Even so, it is almost unbelievable that I am here, I am in Bitlis, that my family has lived here for centuries.

BEDROS.   Well, they certainly welcomed us, they certainly welcomed you—the Mayor, schoolteachers, businessmen, and at least five hundred people. What did you think when you saw them?

BILL.   I thought, well, it's damned nice of the Mayor and all the others of course, and it was pleasant to see their good faces and to hear their good voices, but let's not imagine that I don't know somebody has instructed them to do this.

ARA.   Of course, people don't do things of this kind without authorization, without permission, or without instructions. The Turks in Istanbul and Ankara want to welcome a son of Bitlis on a visit to his ancestral home, even if he is a *giaour*, an infidel, and an Armenian. They think of you as one of themselves, a son of Anadole, as they put it. Nobody says Turkish or Armenian. It wouldn't be polite. But here's Akhmed with tea and so let us refresh ourselves.

AKHMED.   Tell him, tell him, please, he even looks to be one of us.

BEDROS.   He's saying in Turkish tell him he looks to be one of us.

BILL.   Yes, and I must say that all of the young men seemed to be members of my own family, cousins, as I said to the Mayor, and to a few of the boys.

ARA.   Well, the Kurd is like the Armenian, he is like us. Take a sip of this aromatic tea, stir in the sugar, lots of sugar. It will refresh your soul. And of course although it is officially frowned upon to remark that you are a Kurd, almost everybody in Bitlis is a Kurd. There was not one Armenian in the crowd. I can spot one in a flash. Not one, not one, and Bitlis, for centuries called Baghesh, was one of the main cities of Armenia.

BILL.   It still is, as far as I am concerned. Yes, the tea is refreshing. My grandmother Lucintak Garaoghlanian made tea like this. In our house on San Benito Avenue in Fresno we drank tea all day in the winter.

ARA.   And in the summer?

BILL.   We ate watermelon. Well, at any rate, I did, for I do love and need lots of water. Akhmed seems like a decent sort. Is he a Turk? Is he a mixture? He looks like one of us.

BEDROS. We all of us share the same earth and have for a long time, and so we are bound to look like one another, but Akhmed is a Turk.

BILL. Not a Kurd, he certainly doesn't look like the boys in the crowd that met us at the gate to the castle. And what is the castle?

ARA. Akhmed is not a Kurd. He is a member of the minority in Bitlis, a Turk, but he is the owner of a restaurant, and that makes the difference. He serves food and drink to customers, and he wants customers, and so in a sense he is not really very much of anything, he belongs to the nationality of cooks and waiters.

BILL. Seems like a nice guy.

ARA. In a nice time anybody is a nice guy. Who should know that better than you. An American. A writer. A student of the human character. Akhmed will be delighted to have the small sum he charges for his good food, which I will double so that when we come again he will remember us, and of course we shall come this afternoon, for this is the only restaurant in town—well, the only one for travelers.

BILL. Why will you double the sum? Ara, you must understand this is not simple curiosity, I suspect there is something formal in that, a kind of statement to him and to those he talked to that you want known. Am I entirely mistaken or is there something to this? A kind of Bitlis or Kurdish or Turkish or regional tradition?

ARA. Yes, precisely—first his bill will be quite small, not quite enough, second I may double it without offending him, I can't triple it for that would be charity, and he has pride—he will say we are people of sense and courtesy. It is important, even for only one day.

BILL. Well, here I am at last in Bitlis, the birthplace of my father Armenak and my mother Takoohi, and of my father's father Bedros and his mother Hripsime, and my mother's father Minas and her mother Lucintak, and I am drinking delicious sweet tea in a glass made by a sensitive Turk and eating the same flatbread that my mother and my grandmothers have always baked and the same kind of simple white cheese that we have always enjoyed, with some real greens of the meadows of Bitlis, and I don't know what to make of it. I just don't know how to experience so much, that's all. I mean, I like everybody I see here, I feel they are also from people who have long lived in Bitlis, and I don't think at all that surely it must have been their grandfathers who made life so hopeless here that it made Minas say to Lucintak, Get out of here, take the family to America, this place is not fit for us any more, we have had enough. And then he died and she indeed got the family out of there, and that's how I happened to be born in Fresno, instead of here. That's where we were, in short. Or do I like everybody because they made life impossible here for Armenians, which drove my family to California so I could be born there? I mean, I am not confused so much as ignorant. I don't know what is going on, because I really don't know what happened in the first place, a thousand times in the first place. Well, here's Akhmed again, with more tea, now how can you hate a Turk like that. And let's face it he doesn't look especially unlike an Armenian.

BEDROS.   The Turks are a mixed breed, of course. They have little of Asia in their faces these days, except now and then.

BILL.   Mixed with Armenians, you mean?

BEDROS.   Of course. And with whoever else has lived here: Georgians, Circassians, Persians, Jews, Abkhazians, Greeks, Assyrians, Arabs, Syrians, Gypsies, and Kurds, a lot of Kurds. Also, Bulgarians and Romanians and Serbs and Montenegrans and Macedonians—this is a crossroads, and even Africans were brought here to work in harems not only of the Turkish royal families but of tribal chiefs and rich men, and there is good black blood mixed in with all of the others. We have much to do and to see in Bitlis, and we have the time we need, so let everything pile up and let it not begin to mean anything until later, perhaps much much later.

BILL.   Oh, it isn't that it doesn't mean anything right now, it is just that my understanding of its meaning is so inadequate. Why did we leave? More Armenians stayed in Bitlis than left? So why did we leave? Why did my grandfather Minas, dying, charge his comparatively young wife with the hard job of lifting the family out of this place and moving it to America, to California, that is what I want to know. In 1944 in London I knew Arshak Safrastian who worked with the English Consul in Bitlis when Lucintak began to arrange for the family to leave Bitlis, and he told me, Ah, she was a great woman, she understood her world and the people who had the power to permit or not to permit, and she knew who the man was that she must bribe with a gold coin, as a gift, not a bribe, and so she worked miracles. All right, let's say Minas dying said something, so what was it in Lucintak Garaoghlanian's character that made her believe she must fulfill his command? Surely she could very easily have found it more comfortable, more sensible, and much more practical to stay put and to think that perhaps next year or the year after we can go to America, or even she might think that conditions would improve, that the Turkish government would give instructions to the Governor General of the vilayet of Bitlis that the Armenians are to be treasured for their industry and productiveness in all areas of community life, and so there would be no need to get up and go.

ARA. Might there not have been in most of the hearts of the people who left not only Armenia and Turkey but all of Europe a dream of a much better and larger kind of life somewhere else?

BILL. Of course, of course, but so many more Armenians did not get up and go, so why did my family? For if I had lived here, I think I would have left it only for a very good reason. This is the most beautiful place I have ever visited, and I have visited many places.

ARA. It is Bitlis, and to you Bitlis means something it does not mean to anybody else.

BEDROS. Well, we walked through Tsapergor Tagh to your father's house and you were there yourself. What do you think?

BILL. I don't know, I don't know, I mean I really don't know, the Kurd who said he was a small boy when he knew my father, the Kurd who took us to the place where my father had lived with his mother and father and brothers and one sister, he seemed like a decent honest sincere man of, oh, about seventy-four, wouldn't you say? But I don't know, why would there be nothing left of my father's house at the top of that high high place at the end of Tsapergor Tagh, nothing left but a hearth, which of course the good photographer Fikret Otyam made much of, asking me to pose there, and taking many shots. I don't know. Is that where we lived, even approximately? I don't want to be ungrateful to anybody, but I have this feeling that some of this has been arranged. Why is that so?

ARA. It is so because it is so, some of it has been arranged. A son of Anatolia has made a pilgrimage to the city of his ancestors, and so the officials made enquiries and found that the stones in the Armenian Cemetery had all been removed and put into repair work on old houses, or into pavements, every now and then if you look down you will see a piece of a gravestone in the street and on it you will see Armenian words and names: Sarkis Da . . . , and the rest is broken away. Surely you must have noticed by now that wherever we have gone—Ankara, Merzifon, Samsun, Trabizond, Erzeroum, Van, Tatvan, and now Bitlis—we have met with nothing but warmth and high respect—but at Giresun they had a grand fish dinner waiting, and again at Agri just below Ararat, a really excellent lunch—all by plan, of course.

BILL. Surely those restaurants prepare food everyday. For everybody.

ARA. Special food for your table, including the three of us and the three photographer-journalists, Fikret, Ali, and Mehmed. It is desirable for you to remember Anatolia fondly.

BILL. Of course it is, I shall, I'm sure, but why shouldn't it be? And so they have rolled out the red carpet for me. So I must be very grateful, and I am, but I don't know, I have dreamed of seeing the Saroyan houses, and all I saw was a hearth, quite small, set in a kind of hillside. I'm not sure I believe that that hearth was ours at all, or that it is part of any one of the eight Saroyan houses, all of them forming a square with a large community garden enclosed by the houses. I liked everything about the location, at the top, that is, with the grand views of the twin peaks across the Bitlis River, roaring far far below, but I'm not sure it is where the Saroyans had their houses, and that makes a difference in my whole connection with Bitlis. I don't want it to be false, or at any rate not too false.

BEDROS. Well, of course it is always best to have something true, but it is not really possible this time, is it? For we are all of us gone from here. I have made enquiries and the only known Armenian is the old man we met outside the Mayor's office. And his name is no longer Armenian, and the Kurdish boys tease him, because they know he is Armenian and old and lives with only one last hope—to be sent to Beirut, in Lebanon, so that he can die among Armenians.

BILL. Poor old guy, I thought he was really the nearest thing to a real hero I have ever seen. Will you get him to Beirut?

BEDROS. I shall write about him in *Marmara*, and perhaps some people will send in some money for a fund—yes, yes, I will see that he gets to where he can walk among Armenians. In Bourdj Hammoud, in that whole quarter of Beirut, there are only Armenians—almost, even the shops have Armenian names on them. We shall get him there, so that he can die with a sense of being at home again. Even though he was born here, in Bitlis almost ninety years ago. Moughsi Baba, the last of the original Bitlis-tsis.

BILL. But the place is ours. Bitlis is ours. Bitlis is mine. I would come and live here if it were a part of our country. And it will be. I am sure that some day it will again be our true Bitlis.

ARA. Really? How can you feel that way? Sentiment? Wish?

BILL. Well, of course, but look at the place. It needs the Armenians. It will once again be a beautiful and important town in the world. That is why I believe it is even now still ours, and will again truly be ours. It needs us. The others can stay or go as they please, but Bitlis is ours.

ARA. Yes, Bitlis probably does need the Armenians, but so does Moush, which we shall see this afternoon, and so does Van, which we have seen, and so does Dikranagert, or Diyarbekir, and so does Kharpert sometimes called Harpoot, and for that matter who is to say that the Armenians are not needed also by Athens, Rome, Paris, London, New York, Chicago, San Francisco, and Hollywood, especially Hollywood? Yes this is mockery, but there is a certain amount of truth to it, too. What I am saying is, Bitlis needs Armenians, but it will never see them back again.

BILL. I wouldn't be so sure of that.

BEDROS. The Turks were ready to have Bitlis and Moush and Van and Kars and Ardahan and all of the eastern area of Anatolia restored to Armenia after the Second World War, but then America stepped in and made Turkey its frontier against the possible expansion of Communism, but we all know that, don't we? I mean, we all know that history is inferior behavior on behalf of support to a program of profit. Ah, well, now perhaps it is too late . . . forever. But I will get the old man to Bourdj Hammoud in Beirut and he will walk among Armenians and then die feeling that he is home, at any rate. Think of it, a man born in Bitlis must go to another place to believe he has reached home—all because all of Bitlis was made bereft of its real inhabitants, the Armenians.

BILL. So the old man will go home to a strange city which will instantly be home to him because there are Armenians there.

BEDROS. That's it for Armenians in Bitlis, then. He is the last of us, and homesick for what Bitlis was and really is, but now the very graveyard has been demolished and wildflowers are growing there among the planted wheat, and one of our most beautiful churches is the home of cattle and the belltower houses pigeons. And wherever we walk, out where the mineral waters bubble out of great stones, the water which only cows and horses drink, the Turks and Kurds watch us, for they think we have come to dig up the buried gold of our fathers. Good God. You heard them with your own ears, Ara, and I don't know about you, but it made me feel almost glad that we have all of us left here.

BILL.   I am not glad. Bitlis is ours. It is mine. It is theirs, too, they are all inhabitants of Bitlis, and whoever they are, or whoever they become, they are welcome, but it is really ours, it is mine, and I wish to God I could stay. I really want to stay.

ARA.   Well, the Mayor has invited you to stay, to be a guest of the government. And he sounded as sincere as a mayor making such an invitation can be. It might be possible to work something out. You might try it, see if you really think you want to stay, and then make it really work. You have money. And you could buy back the fine stone house built by your grandmother Lucy Garaoghlanian's cousins, Dikran and Aram, near the top of the road through Tsapergor Tagh from the Kurd who runs a fleet of trucks from Istanbul to Turkey continuously and who occupies it. You could give him a little more money than he could afford to reject and own a fine house in that very part of Bitlis that is indeed traditionally yours. And for that matter you could buy the land at the very top of the road which our Kurdish guide insists is where the Saroyan houses had stood and you could build all eight houses precisely as they had once been, and you could be home, you could really be home. It is possible, isn't it?

BILL.   One thing is wrong. There would be no Armenians in town, and I would be a local eccentric. An American-born Armenian writer with enough money accumulated after thirty years of great success comes to Bitlis and decides he must restore the family houses, and in the meantime buys from a rich Kurdish businessman the house of his grandmother's brothers—not cousins. And he moves in—with his typewriter, and stays there, and goes for long walks in the surrounding highlands. A crazy Armenian.

ARA.   Well, what do you think?

BILL.   Get the old man home to a strange city. All the same, Bitlis is ours, it is mine. How or when we shall be here again I don't know, but we shall be, it is clearly indicated—or Bitlis must fall into ruins.

ARA.   That is the general trend in this part of the world, isn't it? Let the Armenians make new cities for a couple of centuries. And I don't mean in Soviet Armenia alone. Everywhere.

BEDROS.   Is Bitlis indeed here, though? Is this the only Bitlis? When you are home in California, in Fresno, in San Francisco, or on the beach at Malibu, are you not also again or still in Bitlis? When you put up a new house on land of your own is not the land and is not the house Bitlis? Let this old Bitlis, or Baghesh, fall into ruins, inhabited by Kurds, and a minority of Turks, whose countrymen have the government and whose name is on the country. Let it fall away to time and become ruins, like the great castle and fort sealed tight all these years, what have we lost, any of us? Do you really love Bitlis, or is it in fact life itself that you love, and your family?

BILL.   Ah, of course there is sense to what you say, my friend, you are an architect and a publisher of the Armenian daily in Istanbul, *Marmara*, named after the body of water down a bit from the Black Sea, and all of your questions I have indeed asked myself many times during the past twenty-four hours, and the past twenty-four days, and twenty-four months, and years, and perhaps centuries, too, for all I know. And the answer to all of these questions is always useless, for by turns and even simultaneously the answer is both yes and no, which is in our very natures to begin with. In other words, I choose to love Bitlis and to believe that it is ours. Of course I choose. I have no choice but to choose. But since I do choose, that is it, is it not, that is the truth of it, I love Bitlis, I believe it is ours, it is mine. Let whoever cares to do so, or must do so, as I must, choose to believe Bitlis is his, not mine, and that will also be so. But I am here, in this place I have heard about all my life, and thought about, and dreamed about, and I know that we lived here, a family in houses, lived here for surely longer than a couple of centuries, and it is that which compels me to choose to love Bitlis and to believe that it is mine. For where we have been is a special kind of place to each of us, let it be the barren wastes of the north, or the steaming hot forests of the tropics, we have been there, and our having been there has done something to the place which has a meaning for us that is past almost all other meanings, such as simple comfort, for instance. In all exterior things my life in America is more comfortable than it is likely to be here in Bitlis, but that does not diminish my connection with the past of my family

here and I seem to find it necessary to choose Bitlis over California
even though I shall forfeit such appealing things as comfort. What
shall I say? I am broken-hearted? Well, I am, although I despise
such sentiments. I feel that I am in mourning, by being here. I feel
that even though our cemetery is gone, I know my dead for centuries
are here, all of those nameless members of my family, all those
young boys and girls and young men and women and old men and
women, they are all here, and are dead, and I am here, and am
not dead, and I feel them, I feel their livingness from when they
were alive, I see them, I hear their voices, I smell them, and God
help me you must understand that I must, I choose to tell the truth,
I see and hear and smell them in the people who are here now, the
living Kurds, who as you know, as I told them when I first saw
them, look precisely like members of my own family as I have seen
them in California, as they are this very minute in California, and
that is a kind of surprise to me, for I am an Armenian, I am not
a Kurd, my people have been Christians for centuries, and I am
a son of Christians, if I have no deep connection with that or any
other formal religion, I am a Saroyan, I am not a member of the
Barzani family, there might be a trickle of Kurdish blood in my
veins, but that is irrelevant and not anything really meaningful, and
yet when I see the Kurds I see my own family, the Armenians, the
Saroyans, and two hours ago in the great field which is the top of
the castle and fort, twice the size of a football field, when the Kurdish
redheaded bard made up a song of welcome, sung to me, to Veelyam
Sar-o-yan, pronounced precisely as the name is pronounced in proper
Armenian. I felt that that man was a cousin at the very least,
somehow, and I know that all of this thinking is only the consequence
of my simply being here at last, and none of my feelings have any
reasonable connection with truth or reality. I want Bitlis, I want
to live and walk and eat and drink and sleep in Bitlis. Tomorrow
will find us on our way to Diyarbekir, or Dikranagert, but I want
to stay in Bitlis—apparently forever. I want to die here and be with
my dead.

ARA.   And what about the Mayor? How do you like him?

BILL.   He seems a nice little man. I like him. I like him just fine.

ARA.   He says he thinks his mother's mother is Armenian.

BEDROS.   Well of course she might have been. Who can say? He isn't.
He is a Turk. He does not speak Armenian. I like him for other
reasons.

BILL. Yes, that's how it always is. The fact is that I have always noticed the similarity of people rather than the differences. There really are no differences worth bothering with on a human level in this part of the world. I mean everybody seems pretty much the same as everybody else.

ARA. You are dreaming. They are not the same. The Armenian is eager to be doing, the Turk is eager not to be—or to be doing something he has always done, something easy that doesn't make him use any real energy or intelligence. I'm surprised at both of you. And you know perfectly well that my work, commercial farming, is with partners who are necessarily either Turkish or Kurdish, as my present partner is, although the Kurdish part of it he keeps to himself, since the government does not want to acknowledge that it has a minority of anywhere from three to six million Kurds. Mountain Turks is the official designation for them. But I refuse to join you in feeling that everybody here is the same. It just isn't so.

BILL. Well, you certainly have had very real opportunities to notice differences. I haven't, and I don't see any. Oh, what they believe, in religion, we know is not what the minorities believe—a Moslem believes one order of thing, and a Christian another, both fairly useful in sustaining them in their daily lives. But after that, they seem to look and act the same.

ARA. It just isn't so. Those happy smiling healthy Kurdish boys and young men you felt were members of your own family mocked and jeered the old man, Moughsi Agha, and specifically as an Armenian, a silly old Armenian, and the old man took it with enormous grace and dignity, ignoring them completely, even when they pushed him—and of course he is not a strong man. They did that because they are young, that's true, but they also did it because they are Kurds, not Christians, not Armenians, and know themselves to be in the majority here, even though officially they are identified as Mountain Turks. There is terrible cowardice in strength, and that is something I have watched in all people, the Americans, the English, the Russians, but it is never so savage as in this part of the world, among these peoples—Kurds, Turks, and their relatives around about.

BILL. Yes, yes, there is no disputing it, you have lived here and know these things, and I have come here, as to a dream, and I guess I want the dream to go right on being beautiful, unreal, and in a way damned foolish. I really don't think the Kurd presented to me by the Mayor as a man who had known my father and all of my family in all of its branches knew any of us at all—but then I still want to believe that perhaps he did. Why would he say he did?

BEDROS.   Well, of course for the importance of it, for he is already a famous man, he has been photographed with you, and his picture will appear in various newspapers and magazines, and why shouldn't he do it? Perhaps he has heard that the Saroyan houses were indeed up at the top where he took you, and the rest of us.

BILL.   Something keeps telling me just the same, that the place he showed me was indeed the place.

ARA.   Well this is certainly Bitlis, the Armenian Quarter was where he took us, and the Saroyans certainly had houses here, so what's the difference if he took you to exactly the right place? It's right enough—for ruins. The only solid house was put up by your grandmother Lucy's brothers Aram and Dikran Garaoghlanian, and another Kurd is the owner and occupant of that house. And if you were to stay here, you would discover that these very pleasant people are even more pleasant than you first imagined—but also liable to be vicious with anybody weak and vulnerable, like the last Armenian of Bitlis, Moughsi Agha.

BILL.   I won't be staying, so I'll never find out for sure, but I still seem to want to believe that all of us here are really one people.

ARA.   Human, yes. Otherwise, no. Absolutely not.

BEDROS.   Well, maybe. Under the right circumstances, who is indeed who? We can be vicious too.

BILL.   Let me look back from this Chevrolet for one last snapshot of Bitlis. Good God, I can't see anything to take away with me forever. It's just this narrow highway out of town, west, and there are these people walking along the road in great strides—Kurds, the nomadic Kurds, father, mother, sons and daughters, eight handsome people. And up here, what's this? Americans with a truck doing work with the telephone and telegraph wires. Christ, they are everywhere, there is not one place I have visited in this world where I haven't soon enough come upon Americans in the Army, the Navy, the Marine Corps, the Peace Corps, the Diplomatic Service, or just availing themselves of the easy life of that particular people and place, and I don't know, I didn't really want them in the crotch and in the armpits and up the ass of Bitlis, too. But there we are, aren't we? Bitlis would very likely right now be a part of Soviet Armenia had the Americans kept their sticky fingers away. I don't know, I find myself deeply saddened to be leaving the place, but also glad to have it behind me. I had to come, I had to see it, I came, I saw it, I am saddened by it, I am glad to be leaving it, but. . .there is more, there is something nagging at me and I don't know what it is. What is it? What is it?

ARA.   Well, if you can't tell us, we certainly can't tell you.

BEDROS.   No, it's quite simple. It is simply that the place was ours for so long, it was yours for so long, it was the home of the Armenians and the Saroyans for so long, and even though you were born far away from it you were really still here, as if you had been born and had lived here, and you came back and everything was in ruins, and even in doubt, you were taken to where your houses were supposed to have been, but the guide was a simple old gangling Kurd who claimed he knew your father, it was not the old Armenian who will soon be going to Beirut to die among his own kind, the last Armenian in Bitlis did not know your father, did not indeed know about the Saroyans at all, for I made a point of mentioning your name many times hoping that he would remember and speak about that, but he didn't, so there are indeed Armenians who lived in Bitlis for centuries but in all that time did not know other Armenians who also lived here for centuries. And so the place, Bitlis, was not really ours alone, it was also theirs, especially the Kurds who are everywhere in the city now and in the surrounding villages, and had you been born here and still a resident here, Armenian, Kurdish or Turkish, Bitlis would not be yours alone, it would also be theirs, and also the traveler's and the invader's and most of all it would be its own self, a kind of strange reality and secret—of course you are confused, but do you think I am not, and my people never came anywhere near Bitlis over the centuries and I was born in Bolis, as the Armenians prefer to put it, Constantinople to the Greeks, and now Istanbul to the people in power. I am just as sad perhaps as you are, and even though I can guess why you are sad, I really don't believe I am willing to confess that I am sad only because I am an Armenian, and our story does not really permit us anything like common simple gladness about our country. It has never been unmistakably ours long enough at one time, I suppose. And that makes me very sad.

ARA.   I am just as Armenian as you are, as both of you are, and I am not sad about that, or about my country, or about Bitlis, or about the city of my ancestors, Kharpert, which we shall visit in a matter of four or five hours, I am glad about it all, we do not need the childish support of a geographical country to enjoy being who we are. We are who we are in other ways and for better reasons than having our own government pushing us around—let other governments, the governments of other peoples, do that. And who really cares or needs to know why an Armenian happens to be sad, going away from Bitlis or going to Bitlis, or going from one room to another in his own house far from Bitlis. An Armenian is sad because of far far better reasons than geography and arrival and departure of himself somewhere geographical, it is the arrival and departure of everything and everybody everywhere that he knows isn't going to improve anything that saddens him. Saddens me, at any rate, and makes me break into song, so sing with me about eating bread and drinking wine, that's all.

HARATCH

A Play in Three Acts

Dear Dikran

    Please xerox
Haratch (2 or 3 copies,
perhaps) so you can return
this copy to keep my record
complete of 1979 Paris New
writing — 7 works I believe.

                    Bill
Fresno Thursday Oct 2 1980

William Saroyan's note of October 2, 1980 to the editor accompanying a copy of the typescript of the play *Haratch* to be used by students in the latter's class, Theater of William Saroyan, at California State University, Fresno. (Courtesy of Dickran Kouymjian)

ՅԱՌԱՋ

"HARATCH"
Journal Arménien
Paraissant trois fois par semaine
Rédaction et Administration : 65, Rue Pascal, PARIS (13)

Ա. ՏԱՐԻ ԹԻՒ 1

ԿԻՐԱԿԻ
2
ՕԳՈՍՏՈՍ
1925

ԳԻՆ 40 ՍԱՆԹ

ԵՐԿՈՒ ԽՕՍՔ

ՆԵՐԿԻՆ ԼՈՒՐԵՐ

ՕՐԸ ՕՐԻՆ

Le Directeur : SCH. MISSAKIAN
Rédaction et Administration : 32, rue de Trévise - Paris 9ᵉ
C.C.P. Paris 1078-63 — R.C. Seine 376.286
Fondé en 1925 — Tél. : PRO. 86-60

ՈՉ ԵԻՄ Է
ՇԱՒԱՐՇ ՄԻՍԱՔԵԱՆ

The masthead and portion of the front page of the first number of *Haratch*, August 2, 1925. Below, the front page of January 27, 1957 announcing the death of the paper's founder and editor, Schavarch Missakian. (Photos courtesy of Arpik Missakian, *Haratch*)

ՅԱՌԱՋ
ԿԻՐԱԿԻ
ՕՐԱՑՈՅՑ
2 - 3
SAMEDI
DIMANCHE
2-3 AOUT
1975

LE NUMERO 1,20 F.

ՕՐԱԹԵՐԹ
ՀՐԱՏԱՐԱԿԻՉ ՇԱՒԱՐՇ ՄԻՍԱՔԵԱՆ

51ՐԴ ՏԱՐԻ — ԹԻՒ 13.360

HARATCH
Le Seul Quotidien Arménien en Europe Occidentale
Directeur : Arpik Missakian
83, RUE D'HAUTEVILLE, 75010 PARIS

— Tél. : 770-86-60 —   Fondé en 1925
C. C. P. Paris 15069-82   571027317 A R.C. PARIS

Fondateur : SCHAVARCH MISSAKIAN

51ᵉ ANNÉE — N° 13.360

1925 - 1975

ՅԱՌԱՋ 50

Նկար՝ Բարգեւ Գասպարեան

«ՅԱՌԱՋ»Ի ԾԻՆՆԱՐԵԱԿԻՆ ԱՌԹԻՒ

The front page of the 50th anniversary number of *Haratch*, August 2-3, 1975. (Photo courtesy of *Haratch*)

Above, Arpik Missakian, editor of *Haratch*, checking a new issue of the paper as it comes off the press at 83 rue d'Hauteville, Paris, in the company of a typesetter (on her left) and printers, late 1975. Below, she is at her desk in the adjoining offices, November 23, 1981. (Photos courtesy of *Haratch*)

Arpik Missakian standing in the office of *Haratch* under the portrait of her father, Schavarch, March 1979. (Photo courtesy of *Haratch*)

The late Krikor Atamian, Saroyan's tailor friend of Paris, reading to him from *Haratch*. Inscribed on the back of the photo is: "Much admiration to Arpik Missakian for her steadfast editing and publishing of *Haratch* the famous Armenian daily of the Missakian family,...June 18, 1969 William Saroyan." (Photo courtesy of *Haratch*)

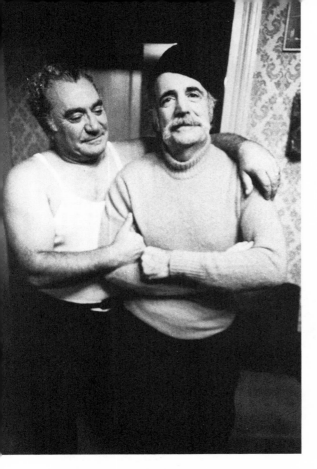

Two of the characters of the play *Haratch*: above, Soviet Armenian writer and editor Harachia Hovannissian with Saroyan in Paris circa 1974. (Photo Ara Güler); and, below, Anoushavan Kapikian, Paris, January 1979. (Photo courtesy of *Haratch*)

More characters from Saroyan's *Haratch*: above, the late Archbishop Serovpe Manougian of Paris ("Bishop Stepan" of the play) officiating at the 75th anniversary ceremony of the Armenian General Benevolent Union before the mausoleum of its founder Boghos Nubar Pasha in the cemetery of Père-Lachaise, Paris, May 10, 1981. To the left, in profile, is Alex Manoogian, Life President of the AGBU, and in the center, Nourhan Fringhian, Honorary President of the AGBU in France. (Photo Dickran Kouymjian) Below, Khachig Tölölyan after a guest lecture for the Armenian Studies Program on his first visit to Fresno, October 5, 1985. (Photo CSUF Armenian Studies Archive)

THE PEOPLE

WILLIAM SAROYAN, *Armenian-American writer living between Paris and Fresno, California*
ARPIK MISSAKIAN, *editor of* Haratch, *the Armenian daily newspaper of Paris*
ZOHRAB MOURADIAN, *48, habitué of* Haratch
KHACHIG TÖLÖLYAN, *Armenian-American professor of English and American literature at Wesleyan College, in Paris on a visit*
SYLVIA, *Armenian-American friend of Khachig*
OLD MAN FROM BITLIS, *88, Dikran Boshbazmanian by name, habitué of* Haratch
HRACHIA, *editor from Soviet Armenia on a visit in Paris*
ZULAL, *writer, teacher, architect, habitué of* Haratch
BISHOP STEPAN, *principal clergyman of the Armenian church in Paris*
COP, *a French policeman*
ANOUSHAVAN KAPIKIAN, *habitué of Haratch*

THE PLACE

The offices of Haratch, *the Armenian daily newspaper of France and Europe at 83 rue d'Hauteville in the tenth arrondissement of Paris.*

THE TIME

A day in the Spring of 1979.

NOTE. The play was written in one act with thirty scenes in Paris between June 23 and July 22, 1979. It has been divided into three acts by the editor.

ACT ONE

SAROYAN. I know I've asked before, but please make allowances for my failing memory, who is the man in that painting above your desk?

ARPIK. I've told you many times. My father.

SAROYAN. You mumble, perhaps that's why I never quite know what you have said. Who? Who did you say?

ARPIK. My father.

SAROYAN. Your father, you say? What does that mean? I mean, who is he?

ARPIK. Schavarch Missakian, the founder of this paper.

SAROYAN. What paper, let us get these things straight.

ARPIK. You know perfectly well what paper: *Haratch*. It means forward.

SAROYAN. In New York Abraham Cahan was the founder and editor of the *Jewish Daily Forward*. Yiddish as a matter of fact. Out of the German language more or less.

ARPIK. Forward is a popular direction.

SAROYAN. You've hung your head and you're mumbling again, what did you say?

ARPIK. I said forward is a popular direction for a patriotic daily, as I am sure the *Jewish Daily Forward* of New York was, and this Armenian daily of Paris is *Haratch*, *Forward*. Schavarch Missakian my father is the founder of this daily paper, and I am the publisher and editor since his death thirty years ago.

SAROYAN. That's a long time.

ARPIK. I got the paper out every day, except Monday, six days a week year after year.

SAROYAN. That takes work. Did your father ask that you do this?

ARPIK. He died of a heart attack suddenly and didn't ask me to do anything, but I suppose it never crossed his mind that his daily paper would die with him, so I kept it going, and one year led to another until now, here we are.

SAROYAN. What do you print in each issue, all these days of all these years, the founding editor so long gone from the scene?

ARPIK. We publish what any patriotic paper publishes. News of the Armenians wherever they happen to be, but especially in Paris, and in Soviet Armenia.

SAROYAN. Who writes all this stuff? Surely the four pages of each issue requires about eight thousand words a day.

ARPIK. We were eight pages for years, and even these days we sometimes go to eight pages.

SAROYAN. Yes, well, who writes all that stuff?

ARPIK. I do, Zulal does. And of course every day to this office comes an old Armenian with another fragment of his memoirs. We have a man from Bitlis who brings us new stuff every other day, but after we had run six or seven of his pieces we told him that was enough, do not write any more memoirs, but he refuses to stop, he brings new memoirs every other day, and I tell him the same thing, go home for God's sake old man, your memories of Bitlis do not help us at all.

SAROYAN. Isn't that a piece of awful rudeness to an old man, surely sincere?

ARPIK. Oh, he's surely sincere all right, but he is also an awful bore.

SAROYAN. Do you mean to tell me that you are able to say of somebody that he is a bore, or of a piece of writing that it is boring?

ARPIK. Oh, yes, I am able to say that.

SAROYAN. Then, others are surely able to say the same thing of your own writing, are they not.

ARPIK. I don't care what they say, I have my paper to get out and I get it out.

SAROYAN. Oh, it isn't that that isn't a commendable achievement, but I am thinking about the basis of deciding what is boring. Is your writing read by your readers?

ARPIK. Sometimes. They write to me if something pleases them. I guess most of my writing is read most of the time. It could be very boring to some of my readers, perhaps especially the younger readers.

SAROYAN. Is it boring to you? Do you enjoy writing it?

ARPIK. It isn't boring, but I don't believe I can say I enjoy writing.

SAROYAN. That's a pity. Enjoy it, or don't write.

ARPIK. Perhaps I enjoy it, but don't know that I do.

ZOHRAB. Arpik Missakian is a man of a woman, and has been since the death of her beloved father. She is much more than just an editor and a writer.

SAROYAN. Yes she is, yes she is indeed.

ZOHRAB.   She might have discontinued the publication of *Haratch* a year after the death of the founder. It is very hard work to get out a daily newspaper. But she knew that the paper is not just a paper, it is many other things.

SAROYAN.   Yes it is, yes it is indeed.

ZOHRAB.   I have been proud and happy to be associated with Arpik these past twelve years and I know her, and I marvel at her wisdom, her fortitude, her intelligence, her kindness, and above all things her steadfast belief in Armenia. She is herself Armenia—in the Dispersion. We would all of us be lost without her. She has kept Armenia alive in our hearts and minds through the writings in the pages of *Haratch*.

SAROYAN.   Yes she has, yes she has indeed.

ARPIK.   Are those words of courtesy or perhaps humor?

SAROYAN.   What sort of humor? How can you ask a question like that. Do you yourself, then, disbelieve what Zohrab has just said? For if you do, you are mistaken, he has spoken the truth, and I have said to myself the very same things he has said to me, to you, to all of us. I met your father here in Paris in 1935 on my way to Russia and to Armenia for the first time. I made a terrible faux pas when at a large reception I asked him and his colleagues: What is it that you want from the young Armenians here? Why don't you let each of them seek out his own life and meaning? Why do you nag at them to be proud Armenians, to work for the re-establishment of Independent Armenia? It is fifteen years now that Armenia has been a part of Russia, let us be glad that we have the protection of such a great nation and people. Now, of course, I spoke sincerely but even while I spoke I knew many old party members were annoyed and even angry and I expected a rebuke, at the very least, but your father took my side and spoke up for my theory and I tried to understand why he did that, for he did not really believe that it was a sound theory.

ARPIK.   You do not remember that I was there, but I was. I was brought up by my father. I worshipped him of course.

SAROYAN.   Well, I do remember that there was a pretty young girl in a white dress who moved near him continuously, and so now all these years later I discover that that girl was you. Well, you still have the same small feet. They have not changed.

ZOHRAB.   Feet, what's feet got to do with what we're talking about?

SAROYAN. Well, nothing special, certainly nothing momentous, but you see everything is related to everything else, and each of us stands on his feet, and it is the manner in which we do so that perhaps identifies each of us. For a person with great and heavy responsibilities, I marvel that Arpik has held up everything so fully on such slender graceful feet. I consider that a matter of considerable worth. So you were that lively intelligent little girl in the white dress in 1935, and here it is almost 1980—amazing.

ARPIK. Yes, I was that little girl, and yes it is amazing, for I have been so busy I sometimes forget all the years that have gone by. As you Americans like to ask, What happened? Well, whatever it was, I have this editorial office, and beyond it I own the printing presses, and the paper is not in debt to anybody. If it does not quite pay its way, it is also not a burden on the community.

ZOHRAB. And there would be no community without the paper.

ARPIK. Well of course there would be the church, but that constitutes a condition that is not quite complete. When there is both the church and the press, we know that we are there, alive, and moving forward.

SAROYAN. *Haratch*, in short. Forward, ever forward. To what?

ARPIK. To not forgetting, to begin with, and after that to whatever the future may bring. I am keeping the Armenian future alive for any possible eventuality, and that could just mean an independent Armenia again.

ZOHRAB. And there's your answer.

SAROYAN. Yes it is, yes it is indeed.

ARPIK. I still am not sure you are not speaking with amusement.

SAROYAN. Believe me, I treasure *Haratch* as much as anybody.

KHACHIG. Well, well, well, hello to everyone here. And who have we with us this time.

ARPIK. Khachig Tölölyan, have you met William Saroyan?

KHACHIG. Everybody has met William Saroyan, everybody believes he knows William Saroyan. I have read your most famous books.

SAROYAN. I like the ones that are not famous.

KHACHIG. That is the way with writers. They are always fondest of those books which the world refuses to honor by reading, even.

SAROYAN. And are you a writer, also?

KHACHIG. In a way, but I earn my living teaching.

SAROYAN. Where?

KHACHIG. At Wesleyan College in Middletown, Connecticut.

SAROYAN.   What do you teach?

KHACHIG.   Oddly enough, English and American literature.

SAROYAN.   Literature? Do you mean writing?

KHACHIG.   Well, the name of the course is in the catalog as English and American Literature.

SAROYAN.   I would like to ask a question that I hope you will not misunderstand. How much do you earn from this work?

KHACHIG.   Fifteen thousand a year. It is not much, but it keeps me going. If I were married and had two or three children, fifteen thousand wouldn't be anywhere near enough, of course.

SAROYAN.   And your father, what does he do?

KHACHIG.   He retired just last year, at the age of sixty-five.

SAROYAN.   Well, what did he do?

KHACHIG.   Well, he was one of two editors of *Hairenik* in Boston for the past twenty-two years.

SAROYAN.   I used to know Reuben Darbinian, but perhaps you know that his real name was Chilingirian.

ARPIK.   Yes, we all know that, but it was traditional for patriotic editors to have a second name, so that they might avoid difficulties over some of their editorials.

SAROYAN.   You haven't changed your name.

ARPIK.   I decided not to.

SAROYAN.   You are your father's daughter, and you did not want his name to be separated from his paper, *Haratch*. Is that right?

ARPIK.   Well, something like that, but there are very few difficulties these days.

ZOHRAB.   Yes, but during the occupation of Paris, the Germans came to you with offers to finance *Haratch*, but you turned them down, and suspended publication during the entire occupation.

SAROYAN.   Really? That seems both heroic and unnecessary, and yet I gather that there were excellent reasons for your decision.

ARPIK.   France has been good to us, to the Armenians in general, and to *Haratch* and Schavarch Missakian and his daughter in particular, I could not accept the courteous friendship of the enemy in France, that's all.

SAROYAN.   Courteous?

ARPIK.   Oh, yes, the Germans were always courteous, soft-spoken, very considerate, and they accepted my own decision without annoyance, or at any rate without apparent annoyance.

SAROYAN. Perhaps they were courteous with the millions of Jews and Catholics and Anarchists and Gypsies they murdered in various hideous ways during the war.

ARPIK. I have spoken with people who have survived those places and some remark that the Germans were unfailingly courteous and others remark that the courtesy was all the more terrifying because there was no place for it among both the powerful and the powerless. And still others remarked the Germans were invariably ugly and brutal. I found them courteous, but I refused to deal with them. I have become a citizen of France, a country I have every reason to love.

SAROYAN. The more I learn about you the more I admire you.

ARPIK. I do my work and live my life.

ZOHRAB. The question is when shall Armenia have its territory restored?

ARPIK. Well, yes, but actually that may not be the question at all. We are still among the living, and we are still a people.

SAROYAN. Well, as long as we are all here, all different kinds of members of the human family, perhaps we can consider the question: What is it that makes us Armenian? I mean, I find that nobody here looks especially Armenian.

SYLVIA. You do, you look exactly Armenian.

SAROYAN. Well, thank you. I'm glad you think so, and I may say you seem to me to look Spanish while your fellow-American, Khachig, looks perhaps French, perhaps Italian, perhaps even German.

KHACHIG. I have been told I look Russian.

ARPIK. Zohrab is from Moush, is it possible you can say he does not look Armenian?

SAROYAN. Yes, it is, for if we were to find him in Cairo among Egyptians we might instantly believe he was one of them, or in London, among cockneys, we might believe he was one of them.

ZOHRAB. From Egypt to England, that's quite a jump. I am an Armenian.

SAROYAN. Yes, we all are, but let me make the case even more complicated to our way of thinking—any of us in Turkey, in Istanbul, or in Ankara, or Samsun, or Trabizond, could be taken for Turks, could we not?

ARPIK. Well, could we? I am not that sure, but perhaps we could. Didn't one of us once say that our eyes give us away? The Turks look for our eyes and know that we are who we are.

SAROYAN. Many Turks have Armenian eyes, I've seen them, and I would have sworn they were Armenians who had decided for good sensible reasons to pass themselves off as Turks—and they had my sympathy if not admiration.

KHACHIG. Well, some of them surely had Armenian blood, an Armenian grandmother, for instance.

SAROYAN. Not a grandfather, or a great grandfather? Did no Armenian boy make a Turkish girl pregnant?

ARPIK. They say it happened all the time, but the Armenians being Christian themselves one by one, the boys and men, kept it to themselves or pretended that it hadn't happened, or denied it. The Turk has long since taken on the appearance of the European, especially in the cities, whatever he may still be in the villages and remote places. Even there, we don't see much of Asia in his face, although now and then we do see a trace of Asia in an Armenian face. The question is: What is it we are eager to find out from this line of thought?

SAROYAN. I am thinking that anybody can be a member of any race he chooses, for one reason or another.

KHACHIG. Only the American black man is denied that privilege—if he is indeed truly black. I know many blacks who are actually chocolates, cocoas, tans, and other shades of skin common among all peoples, but they go right on choosing to be black. I once asked one of them why, and he said, Well, my father and mother are rather blacker than I am, and some of my brothers and sisters are rather less black, and we are all happy not to repudiate one another. It makes sense. If you were permitted to choose, would you choose something other than Armenian?

SAROYAN. No, because it wouldn't help, and besides Armenians are as interesting as any other people, although I find the Basque people appealing to my sense of uniqueness, and then I am very fond of what the Irish have done in the English language, and in a sense to that language, and I am everlastingly amazed and delighted by the achievements and the variety among the Jews. I go back again and again to the theory that they are God's chosen people. If they aren't, nobody is. But I really wouldn't care to be anything other than what I am, which is at least nine-tenths not known to me. I am not my father and not really too much like him, but I am of his son, if you understand what I mean. I find that rather worth a lifetime of acceptance, and then it is too late in any case, isn't it? How about you?

SYLVIA. Me? Why me? Why not Arpik, the only other woman in this group?

SAROYAN. All right, Arpik. Would you rather be something else?

ARPIK. Oh, I have given it thought. Who hasn't? We are a great people, but we are also a terrible people in many ways. Still, I prefer to be both great and terrible and Armenian. Perhaps it's laziness. Aren't we all lazy?

SAROYAN. Yes, indeed we are, and birth settles it, but I always believed I was free to be the kind of Armenian, the kind of self I have become, and while you might instantly feel I should not have bothered, I must confess I had no choice, I had to bother, and that also is Armenian, don't you think?

KHACHIG. As a teacher of English and American literature, at the college level, I hope I may introduce a note of earnestness into this haphazard but pleasant and certainly unexpected display by you of warmth and friendship toward one and all.

ARPIK. Did you understand what he said? His Armenian is excellent, if a little unfamiliar.

SAROYAN. He wants to ask me a question, I suspect. Please do. But I warn you that although I have been answering questions since my first book came out in 1934, as if I really had answers, the fact is that I have no answers at all, certainly none that you yourself don't have, and I mean especially you, because you are a professor. What is your question?

KHACHIG. Oh, it is not that kind of question at all. It is another kind, a nationalist question, it is a question of perhaps some edge of impoliteness, even, although I shall not ask it in any such spirit.

SAROYAN. Yes, well, what is it? I am here, and as we see my mouth is in good working order. I believe I shall be able to respond with words of some sort to your question. Just ask it, please.

KHACHIG. How does it happen that you have not learned to read and write in the Armenian language?

ARPIK. We have all asked him that question, and he has made a different answer every time. The only thing we know is that he is not able to read or write in the Armenian language.

KHACHIG. Yes, but why hasn't he learned to do so? That is the question.

SAROYAN. The answer is this: I don't know.

KHACHIG. Is that all?

SAROYAN. No, there is more, and there is so much more that I am not sure I could not speak for the rest of this day making known that vast body of more. I suppose you are hopeful that I shall make some kind of special answer. There is none, I am afraid. It is not any of it special. It is just so. Perhaps I did not learn to read and write in the Armenian language because I was so concerned about both reading and writing expertly, excellently, in my own way, in the English language. Does that satisfy you as being a proper answer?

ARPIK. Well, whether it does or not, it is your answer this time, and it is a new answer. I remember two dozen other answers, and each was different. Any answer is a proper answer, of course, but what we are probably trying to say is, alas, if only you had become an Armenian writer.

KHACHIG. No, not really, although there is that element in the question. I am thinking of several other aspects of the matter. You will not be offended, I hope, if I suspect you chose English over Armenian because you noticed in Fresno that the only readers of Armenian were readers of the Armenian papers, full of editorials, and the readers were all old men.

SAROYAN. There was an element of that in my choice, most likely, had there been an element of choice in the matter at all, and I am afraid there wasn't. I was taught English at school, I was not taught Armenian. And after I began to be a writer I believe I took the attitude that if I wrote well in English I was at the same time writing well in Armenian.

ZOHRAB. And in French and Italian and Spanish and Russian and German. English is translated ten times to one time for Armenian. He has said, hasn't he, that he is an Armenian writer. The Americans and the English have noticed that he has said that. Not long ago an Englishman writing about modern Armenia has put him among Armenian writers, even though his working language is English. As far as I am concerned, when I learned about that, there was no longer any question about the matter. He is, he was, he always has been an Armenian writer, and always will be.

SAROYAN. Well, I don't think we really need to make too much of it, for if the truth is told, the real truth, the hard truth, I am both an American and an Armenian writer, and I am neither, I am only the writer I am. I write Saroyan, and there is an old joke among various sophisticated American critics and readers that my writing needs translating from the Saroyan in order to be understandable. I don't mind that joke, although I consider my writing very simple and very easy to understand, although it does concern itself with every complicated aspects of mortality.

KHACHIG. I mean, I wish I might have the simple experience of reading a new piece of writing by you, written in our own language, that's all.

ZOHRAB. Well perhaps I'll go home now, I get tired earlier than I used to, since my heart operation.

SAROYAN. What did you think? Did you think it would be successful? Are you all right? I mean, why did you have a heart attack in the first place? You're very thin, but when I first saw you I imagined it was because you had made a point of it, not eating bread and all that, but now what are you permitted to eat? Are you all right? Are you frightened?

ZOHRAB. Which question shall I answer first.

ARPIK. Go home and rest. He doesn't expect you to answer any of them.

ZOHRAB. Well, I think I want to answer some of them. I mean, I have thought about all of them, and talking about it may be a good thing.

ARPIK. In public, like this? In front of the whole world. You're a fearless man, so how will you confess to all of us the simple truth that you are terrified of dying, even now, even after the long difficult operation, the removal of a strong vein from a leg and the fixing of it in the heart—and then the dangerous time immediately afterwards, many die then, you know, so you are alive and putting back some of the flesh that was worn away, are you sure you want to tell us you are able even to cry to yourself secretly about the possibility of suddenly dying and being gone from here?

ZOHRAB. You know everything. It is true, but there is more. And yes, I want to confess it in front of the whole world.

BITLIS. Excuse me, excuse me, I have only brought some more memoirs of Bitlis, do not interrupt anything, go right ahead, I am in no hurry, at eighty-eight years of age there is no hurry at all, and I thank God that my pen is still healthy and that there is this daily Armenian paper in Paris, in the world, to publish my memoirs of Bitlis. Who was speaking when I came in? Was it you, Zohrab? Please go on.

ZOHRAB.   Yes, it was me, and I was invited by everybody to confess exactly how I feel about my heart attack, the long surgery that followed, and the feelings I have about myself and life and the world and you and Armenia the three months since.

BITLIS.   How do you feel? Well, you surely don't feel sorry you're alive, I don't know much, but I know that much, and let us not forget that I never went to school, I taught myself to read and write, and I have done both for almost fifty years, for I didn't finally start to read and write until I was almost forty. What things are in writing, what amazing things can be found in books and in newspapers like *Haratch*. Arpik, what a great responsibility you have to all Armenians in the world dispersion.

ARPIK.   Yes, and perhaps I owe it to them not to publish any more of your memoirs. You are not as great a writer as Krikor Narekatsi, you know.

BITLIS.   Of course not. Who is? I read him and read him, and know what a great people we must be to produce a soul so vast and fierce and loving.

ZOHRAB.   The question is, when did he die? And the reason I ask is: night and day I ask myself how much time is left for me, to breathe. I am forty-eight, how old was Narek when he died, surely you know Arpik.

ARPIK.   He died young but not too young, and in any case we do not know for sure. From his writing we know that as long as he was alive and wrote his lamentations he was a man who wrestled with God, demanding that he too must have at least a tiny speck of God's enormity and truth.

BITLIS.   How well put, Arpik. How sweetly you employ our beautiful tongue.

ZOHRAB.   Death has come home into me, and I am not yet on good terms with it. Did Narek write about that? If so, show me the place and let me read it and study it. I am sorry, but I don't know how to die, and you will please forgive me—I'm all right, I'm all right, just let me blow my nose—I just don't want to die, that's all.

KHACHIG. I know a man in Boston who had the same piece of surgery twelve years ago and he is in better health than ever before. You're not going to die.

ZOHRAB. God bless you, Khachig. I believe you, but Death is in me, Death is with me, that is the confession I want to make, and Death enjoys making me cry, even in public as I just did. It makes me terribly ashamed to have these weak emotions, but I do have them. If we were at war and I was to die for Armenia, that would be another story entirely. But to die in a time of peace, it is terrifying I must tell you. My sleep every night is unbearable. Well, well, I'll go home now—and die. But if I don't you'll see me here again tomorrow afternoon. Do not die while I am gone.

ARPIK. Hrachia, we were just talking about you. Where have you come from this time? How is everybody in Erevan? How long will you be here?

HRACHIA. You were not talking about me, Arpik, but thank you, I know it is only an expression of welcome, and I believe I know all of these people one way or another. They are Armenians, at any rate. I have come from Erevan by airplane. I arrived last night and am staying at the home of the tailor Agamian, he is such a good friend, he could not leave his work just now, so I told him I would follow his map and find this place, but it was not easy, I do not have a military mind, I am poor at maps, everybody is very happy in Erevan, the sun is happy, the moon is happy, the streets are happy, we are all of us writing poems like mad.

SAROYAN. The sun and moon and streets are writing Armenian poems?

HRACHIA. Oh, yes, although we are doing the actual writing for them, because only our streets know the Armenian language, while the sun and moon know all languages but have got them all tangled up, good God, isn't there a drink of whiskey, there was always a drink of whiskey at *Haratch*.

KHACHIG. I will pour drinks for everybody. And what about our sheep, are they happy?

HRACHIA. An allegorical question, I presume. Our sheep are all happy, and healthy, and the lambs play and jump about, and the mothers and fathers standing in deep green grass look at their lambs and then at one another and they say, Well, we are sheep, so what? It's better than being shishkebab. Thank you for the whiskey. Here's to Armenia, here's to Soviet Armenia, here's to the Armenians in the Diaspora, here's to *Haratch*, here's to all of the Armenian newspapers in the Diaspora, here's to sheep, here's to shepherds, here's to sailors and poets and rug peddlers and revolutionaries and professors and little boys and girls trying to understand what it means that they are only Armenians instead of English, French, Russian, German, or Italian. Well, I have told my own children when they were little of course that it means we are the greatest people in the world—and I have said this because I know we are no greater than any other people, but we are also no less great than any of them. Who are they, after all?

SAROYAN.   Yes, of course, they are only Armenians, also, under another name. But I must know more about the poems. Are the stones and rocks of Armenian not writing poems?

HRACHIA.   Ah, yes, of course, always and always, sometimes I think about our great country, no bigger than a big vineyard in Fresno, you yourself said that to me in Erevan a couple of years ago, and I ask myself why has God given us this rocky, dry, terrible place instead of Switzerland, for instance. I'm sure you have all been to Switzerland, well, I have too, and when I say it I very nearly burst into tears because it is so beautiful, so serene, so green, so grassy, so sweet, so pure, so clean, so fresh, and all of the other things that are easy and right—and then, suddenly, I realize that all of Switzerland is wrong, it is wrong, and everything in our little country, every rock, every stone, every mountain is right, and I'll tell you why, too. Because it forces us to work very hard to bring from under or around or above the rocks a little grass for the sheep to eat, a little wheat for our lovely bread, a little literature for our excited young minds and our tired old souls. God gave us our little geography so that we would have to work hard for our daily bread and for our poems down through the ages. I wrote a poem in my heart and head while I was lost trying to follow Agamian's map, and I want you to hear it, but alas I have forgotten it. Something about the seductive beauty of Paris and how it is an outrage to my soul—but that isn't it at all. It is good to see you all.

SAROYAN.   Hrachia, you are heavier now than when I saw you in Erevan a few years ago. Why is that?

HRACHIA.   Oh, I like to eat and as we know I like to drink. That is the truth not just about me, but about all of the poets of Armenia, excepting the women. I must have much bread everyday and much whiskey—well, for us it is Armenian cognac; they say it is one of the best in the world, although I will not turn down a drink of vodka or gin or anything else that is being poured. Yes, I am now almost 150 kilos. How many pounds is that?

KHACHIG. More than three hundred, but let me pour whiskey into your glass again.

HRACHIA. You are a thoughtful lad, and the whiskey is my very soul. Thank God we are here, wherever this is.

BITLIS. Excuse me, excuse me, dear friends. I must go home. It is a beautiful experience for me to be among you, but I must go home now and quickly write what you have said and how you have said it, and then I must rest and have a meal of *bulghour* pilaf with yogurt, and then go to sleep. May I leave this new manuscript of further memoirs?

ARPIK. You may leave it, but I cannot publish it.

SAROYAN. Why not, really? Is everything that you do publish really better than what this man from Bitlis writes?

ARPIK. Yes, it is. He is not a writer.

SAROYAN. How can you say that? I can see his handwriting on that manuscript. It is neat and clear. It has been my experience that when a writer uses a neat, clear handwriting his writing is almost always quite good. My friend from Bitlis, would you be good enough to read the first few words of your manuscript?

ARPIK. Oh, Lord, now what?

SAROYAN. I apologize to you for this intrusion, but I really must hear him read a little of his writing. I believe it must be good. I believe I could swear it. Yesterday Zulal read to me his brilliant essay about the poetry of the late Harout Gostandian, and I knew he was saying very good things about that man whom I met for a moment two years ago at the big patriotic meeting in Marseilles, but I must confess that I felt the writing was much too literary for a daily newspaper, and I know Zulal himself will not be offended by what I am saying.

ZULAL. I write like a teacher, I suppose. Yes, I demand that my writing appeal to the very highest order of sensibility in myself and therefore very possibly in yourself, or somebody else. I don't know, really.

SAROYAN.   Your writing didn't tell me enough about the man himself, and that to me was what I most needed to know, especially after you had quoted from three or four of his rather puzzling poems. Let's permit this good man from Bitlis where he was born eighty-eight years ago to read the first sentence or two of his new manuscript. Will you, then, sir?

ARPIK.   He doesn't know the language, for heaven's sake.

SAROYAN.   How could he possibly not know the language and fill seven or eight sheets of paper with such fine handwriting. It is all words, and if they are simple, if they are simple, isn't that really what we ask of writing?

ZULAL.   Yes, it is, provided the simple words say something that is not simple, that is profound, that is the test of great writing, I think.

BITLIS.   I must go, the Metro ride requires an hour, and the walk to each station, here and there, takes another half hour at least, I am getting both hungry and tired. Please accept the manuscript and publish it.

ARPIK.   I'm sorry, I really can't do that. I mean, various readers have asked me about these memoirs of Bitlis—after all, we have published a dozen or more during the past two years, and perhaps that is enough.

SAROYAN.   Well, before you go, sir, please read the first sentence or two.

BITLIS.   My father was a shoemaker who every evening read the new poem he had written that day, and my mother was the daughter of a shoemaker who never failed to shake her head in admiration for the poem my father had written. She always said, Oh, it is good, it is the best yet. Good night, then, and thank you all.

SAROYAN.   You don't like that writing? Or is it the old man himself that you don't like.

ARPIK.   We live in a terrible world. Do you really believe I should find space in the paper for such writing?

SAROYAN.   Yes, I do. Make space for it. Are there any others who come here with writing?

ARPIK.   Dozens of them, and all of it is memoirs, written as if by farmers and villagers who are amazed that they are able to write at all. There is really no point to the stuff. These are not great men.

SAROYAN.   I think they are, and indeed you will surely forgive me for saying so, I do not think the great men are great men, the men you believe are great. These are the people and even their absurdities are great.

HRACHIA. He's right, he's right, you know, but where's the bottle? I must have more to drink. American, writer, friend, his writing is useless, I must agree with Arpik. What good are dead memoirs with life exploding all around us?

SAROYAN. As good as good might ever be.

ARPIK. Well, it is not my responsibility to the nation to publish the memoirs of every old Armenian in the diaspora, even if there is something special in every piece of writing these old people bring me.

SAROYAN. What about old women? Do they not write memoirs?

ARPIK. They do, but the women who write memoirs are indeed somewhat entitled to do so, for they are women who were teachers, for instance, or medical doctors, or scientists, or simply poets and novelists and writers of history or drama, not the daughters of the wives of shoemakers in Bitlis.

HRACHIA. Well, I think you are forgetting one simple fact—but let me first sip a little more of this new whiskey—and that fact is this: we speak about the people all our lives, the nation is real only in its people, and of course by people we mean all of the people, including professors but there are many more shoemakers than professors and so we ought not to deny the shoemakers or their sons and daughters the right and honor of letting us know what is in their hearts and minds. Our publications belong to all of our people, not just to professional poets and writers, do you agree?

SAROYAN. Well, I don't disagree. Our publications belong to whoever writes, at all. But publications have editors, and editors must decide what they want to go into their publications.

HRACHIA. In Armenia, at home, we do not have any problem of that kind because all of our writers are so lazy that anything they finally bring us we urgently need and we quickly put into print.

SAROYAN. Are there any old men from Bitlis, Sassoun, Van, Diyarbekir, Moush, or any of our other cities who bring you memoirs?

HRACHIA. Do you know it is a very strange fact that there are these men and they do write memoirs and yet they do not bring these memoirs to our publications.

ARPIK. Of course they don't. They are afraid to. You are the
government. *Haratch* is not the government. *Haratch* can criticise
the government. You cannot criticise the government. The old
writers of memoirs are afraid you will punish them for writing their
memoirs the way they write them. Everybody has memories but
under a severe government the people are not quite sure about what
they may remember and what they had better forget. Here in Paris
in the French diaspora our old men remember what they remember
in innocence, at any rate. It is repetitious and boring but it is at
least uninhibited, they do not ask themselves if by remembering
a lullaby that their mother sang to them they are being nationalistic
and, if so, could perhaps be punished for that reason.

HRACHIA. There is nobody in any part of the world who may not be
said to be nationalistic. Our neighbors the Georgians are nationalistic,
and our neighbors the Azerbaijanians are nationalistic, but there
is no harm in it, for we are all of us in the, the large family of
Marxist-Leninist socialist countries with our capital in Moscow,
we are all of us brothers and sisters, and we work for the liberation
of the entire world, for the deliverance of all people from the tyranny
of imperialism.

SAROYAN. For God's sake, Hrachia, are you drunk, already, or
what?

ARPIK. He's drunk but not from two drinks of whiskey, he's drunk
from Marxist-Leninist propaganda which as we all know has been
out of date for the past forty years or more, but especially out of
date the past ten years. Do you agree, Hrachia?

HRACHIA. I disagree, and so does everybody else here, even you,
Arpik. We like to talk as we meet and drink and look at one another
and thank God that we are still alive, that we are once again enjoying
our common Armenian mortality—a roomful of Armenians, most
of them writers, is something to make us burst forth with many
words of many kinds. I am sorry you have all fallen into the error
of believing that chaos is better than order, that capitalist injustice
with useless freedom is better than orderly socialist justice with
responsibility met by all of the people—but all right, all right, we
are Armenians. And I lift my glass to our reality.

KHACHIG. And so do we, but we cannot pretend that things are so
simple.

HRACHIA. But they are, they are. I write a poem, I become a member of the Writers Union, I publish a book of poems, I become the President of the Writers Union, what could be simpler than that?

SAROYAN. Well, not writing a poem and becoming a member of the Union.

ACT TWO

SYLVIA.   A question, please, and please forgive me, I am enjoying this extraordinary situation, so many kinds of Armenians in an editorial office of a daily paper, but if I do not ask this question now, I suppose I will never ask it, and I do really believe I ought to know the answer to the question. Arpik, you have been getting out the daily paper founded by your father about fifty years ago, and all of the rest of you have been Armenians all of your lives, and you have been very much concerned about what you call The Armenian Case, so please tell me, I must know, what is it exactly that Armenians want?

KHACHIG.   What a silly question, my dear. I thought my prolonged and detailed discussions of our history gave you the answer.

ZOHRAB.   No, no, let us not be impatient with the pretty young lady. Your question is not only sensible, it is very timely, and we must answer it.

HRACHIA.   I do not disagree with that theory, but let me remark that there is no question, there never has been any question as to what we want.

SYLVIA.   Yes, but what is it?

SAROYAN.   Well, it is surely not for me to say, I am an American, but among other things I do seem to see a profound longing in the Armenian soul for revenge, and this is something that I think is really useless and ought not to condition our thinking. There is no revenge. Or if there is, we have already had it.

ZOHRAB.   How, may I ask? How have we had our revenge for the two million Armenians killed by the Turks?

SAROYAN.   Well, by our survival and by the variety of our achievements in all branches of human activity, both in the diaspora and in Soviet Armenia. And by the comparative lassitude of the Turks. In all of the years since 1922 and the crime upon Greeks and Armenians at Smyrna, since the establishment of the New Turkey by Ataturk, with the whole Anatolian peninsula in which to flourish, the Turks have done virtually nothing with their independence, their freedom, their security, their magnificent opportunities. Isn't that revenge?

ZOHRAB.   No, not really, the Turk is the same Turk he has always been. Nobody expects very much of him excepting perhaps more barbarity.

SAROYAN. Well, let us see about letting the young lady know what we want, then, for it may be that the time has come, or is approaching when we shall be asked that question by the world itself and by the Turks themselves.

ZOHRAB. We want back our country. Armenia. All of it. Arpik, tell her.

ARPIK. Well, the fact is that we really do not have an official body of people to speak for us, to answer that simple question, and it is very understandable that we do not. In the diaspora we have only Armenian communities here and there, around a church and newspaper, but we do not have elected representatives, we have a group of Armenians who are swiftly becoming half-Armenians and quarter-Armenians. As for the situation in Soviet Armenia, I am sure Hrachia will not be offended if I suggest that we receive instructions on all matters from Moscow, and there is no reason to expect Moscow not to continue the policy of not offending Turkey, because Turkey is very useful to Russia both as a neighbor and as a possible member of the Russian family of nations. There is a rather strong Turkish Communist underground and both intellectuals and students are members of it. We know what we want, but we also know we have no way of effectively asking for it, legally, or demanding it not necessarily by means of force, or war, but by the support of nations larger and more powerful than Turkey. Our position is perhaps quite sensibly the position for which Armenians have a certain amount of talent—to be patient, very patient, to watch and to wait, and to keep all Armenians more or less in readiness.

SYLVIA. In readiness to do what? Am I supposed to be in readiness?

ZOHRAB. Yes, you are, by being an Armenian maiden, and soon very probably by taking an Armenian husband and having Armenian children. That is how it is in the Diaspora, whatever it may be in Soviet Armenia.

HRACHIA. We also are being patient, and watching and waiting, what else could we possibly be. Armenians are nothing if not worldly and in a certain sense helplessly wise in the ways of the world. If we wait long enough there is bound to be change, and this time it will be in our favor. I swear it, and please be good enough to fill this glass again.

SYLVIA. That is no answer, at all. Well, so be it, then—children.

SAROYAN.   I am speechless. I don't know what to say. Silence has
fallen upon my soul. I cannot open my mouth. And surely I did
not live to be seventy-one years old in order to suddenly fall silent,
but it is true, I have fallen silent, I am speechless, I have nothing
to say.

ARPIK.   Then who is it saying what you just said?

SAROYAN.   That was my father.

HRACHIA.   Ah, Saroyan, Saroyan, what a jokester you are. Pour into
this glass, please, Khachig American. Why have you fallen silent?

SAROYAN.   Why not? I mean, I find that a conversation fascinates me
only if I do most of the talking, but surely a time must come when
somebody else must take over. Zohrab? Khachig? Arpik? Sylvia?
Or should we rush about in the streets in pursuit of the old man
with memories of Bitlis and bring him back? I don't know. I'm at
a loss. Somebody say something right.

KHACHIG.   Right is right and right is wrong, and wrong is wrong and
wrong is right, do you like that sort of Gertrude Stein talk?

SAROYAN.   Am I to understand that you know the work of Gertrude
Stein?

KHACHIG.   Of course, have you forgotten that I teach English and
American writing.

ZOHRAB.   Do you teach his American writing?

KHACHIG.   Yes, some of it; not all, but surely enough.

SAROYAN.   And I know the works you teach: *The Human Comedy*,
My Name Is Aram, and perhaps *My Heart's in the Highlands*, my
first play.

KHACHIG.   Yes, but also some of the short stories in your first book.

SAROYAN.   I am speechless. Say something else, then, somebody,
anybody.

SYLVIA.   We were talking about what we want, and we did not come
to the end of that question at all. So what do we want?

ZOHRAB.   Death, they say death is the one thing that everybody alive
wants but is afraid to confess, and I remember that when I was near
death in the hospital I did not want death at all. I hated it. I thank
God that I did not die, and I also thank God that when I get home
there will be good Armenian food to eat—*bulghour* pilaf and
madzoon. I love that dish.

SAROYAN.   How good it is not to die, is that it, Zohrab?

ZOHRAB.   Yes, that is it.

SAROYAN. For yourself, or for all of us, and I mean for Armenia?

ZOHRAB. Most of all for Armenia. We know each of us must die, but by now I think we also know that Armenia shall not die.

SAROYAN. It is so, it is really so, because we might have died long long ago if we were ever going to do so, and we didn't, so we cannot be expected to die now. One one one, and one by one, each of us here will give over and gladly, I believe, but Armenia will always be there, both as geography and as a living culture, don't you think?

ARPIK. That's what *Haratch* has been saying these fifty long years.

SYLVIA. Well, then if we don't know what we want, do we know what we don't want? I mean, surely something or other is sharply and clearly established in our hearts and minds, and so let us find out what it is.

HRACHIA. Well, you are an American, I should guess, although it may be that you were born in Europe, but let me ask you this simple question: Would you be willing to uproot yourself from America and go and live in Armenia, which I know you are instantly going to call Soviet Armenia, and quite rightly, for that is its full name, it is a part of the great Soviet Russian family of nations, and I for one am proud and glad that because of Russia we have had these past fifty years in which to catch our breath and to become not just a good member of the family of Marxist-Leninist Socialist nations, but real Armenians, for is there anywhere in the Dispersion a group of Armenians that we can truthfully say is more Armenian than the generality of the Armenians in Soviet Armenia. I think not, for the coloration of Armenians in America is American, and in Mexico and in the Argentine and in Brazil, it is Spanish, and here in France, it is French, and so on, but in Armenia everything is Armenian, and if that doesn't compel us to thank God than nothing can. Are you willing, then? Will you give up your life and meaning in America and go to Armenia?

SYLVIA. No, I don't think so.

HRACHIA. I was quite sure that would be your answer.

SYLVIA. But I would go to Armenia for a visit, possibly a rather long visit, perhaps six months, possibly a year.

HRACHIA. Yes, that is happening quite a bit among our young people from all over the world, and we pay them to come and study and learn and think and feel and write, and I consider this one of the best of all of our investments in the future. But you must know that there have been quite a few Armenians who have been young, but not immature, who have come to Armenia and have chosen not to return to the Dispersion, except perhaps for a visit. One out of perhaps one hundred, of course. But that one may be the one we want and most urgently need.

SYLVIA. Does that mean then that you consider the ninety-nine who go back to where they live in the Dispersion are poor Armenians, and good riddance?

HRACHIA. Oh, no, my dear, we want Armenians in the Dispersion who have lived in Soviet Armenia and have become acquainted with the Armenian people at home, safe at home these past fifty years. The two need one another. Soviet Armenia needs all Armenians of the Dispersion, we have always said so, that is why long ago we established the Committee for Cultural Relations with Armenians Abroad, and why we are forever paying for students to come and go to school in Armenia, and for distinguished Armenians in all fields to come and meet us at home, and why we send our people out to the Armenians of the Dispersion, to meet them and to know them, and to accept their hospitality, which as we know is lavish everywhere, for we are a hospitable people. We used to find it necessary to consider *Haratch*, for instance, an enemy, because it was the official paper of the Armenian Revolutionary Party, the Dashnaks, but that day has come and gone, I am happy to say, and how glad we all are in the arts and sciences in Soviet Armenia that we have Arpik Missakian in full charge of this remarkable daily, which, without forfeiting any of its own political beliefs, does not attack the reality of Soviet Armenia. This resolution was in my opinion one of the most significant that came to pass in Armenia, in Soviet Armenia, in the ungeographical Armenia of all Armenians in the Dispersion. We no longer need to look at one another with doubt and suspicion and anxiety and fear. I am here both as a member of the Party in Erevan and as an Armenian, I might even say as a World Armenian, for although I am only the editor of *Sovetakan Grakanoutiwn*, or *Soviet Literature*, and a poet who began to publish in books thirty years ago, my government assigns me to visits wherever there are colonies of Armenians, and I gladly go, and enjoy getting to know more and more Armenians of all ages and classes, rich and poor, and please put a little more whiskey in this glass, Khachig lad.

KHACHIG. I thought you would never ask.

HRACHIA. Ah, we enjoy a laugh, too, don't we, and even if you, Arpik, were to write an editorial naming me as a terrible drunk, believe me, my government would not feel that I had disgraced myself or my government.

SAROYAN. But there is this, there is this, my friends, fellow Armenians, and this is the big thing, there is death, we are dying, this moment of our being together in this editorial office of *Haratch* is real at this living moment, but we are all dying, and the next thing we know we shall be dead and forgotten, and something out of this moment shall survive us, or not, and what are we going to do about that simple fact? Right now there are four or five million of us in Soviet Armenia and in the Dispersion, but all of these living will be dead in a hundred years, even those who were born a moment ago, for very few people live beyond one hundred years, but something out of our lives, their lives, will hang on, will be in the new Armenians both in Armenia and in the Dispersion, and the question is this, what will this something be, and will it be worth any of us new Armenians to want to preserve, to keep, to have, to work upon some more, to hand to our kids? This is the question.

ARPIK. This is not the question, but let us say that it is the question, perhaps I may ask this question: What is it that any of us, Armenian, Turk, Greek, Jew, Russian, or American, has received from his parents, and what is it that any of us has passed along to his children? Isn't it all rather haphazard, and something that either happens of itself or doesn't happen?

KHACHIG. We are getting into dimensions of dispute, of course, and Armenians are always at home in that dimension. We want to hand down our language, but alas, Hrachia, my friend, Russian-Armenian is not really our language, it does not have the power and wealth of our language, you have all of you done us a terrible injustice by letting the Russian influence damage our language.

HRACHIA. There are linguists and philologists who take the opposite view. They feel that Soviet Armenian is far superior to what is known as Western Armenian, and all it needs is a great writer to demonstrate this truth.

KHACHIG. But you have at least five hundred members of the Writers Union in Erevan, are not any of those writers great?

HRACHIA. Every one of them is great, but not great enough.

SAROYAN. Why not? Why isn't there a truly great writer in our Armenia?

HRACHIA. You cannot vote a great writer into coming to pass. He comes to pass or not, and there is still no way to arrange for it to happen. I always believed I was a great writer—until I published a dozen books and read them and became fifty years old, and then I knew I was not a great writer at all, and I began to get fat, for which I make no apologies at all, it is good for me to drink and get fat. For a long time I really believed I was great and would one day demonstrate this truth, but it didn't happen.

KHACHIG. I remember talking with an Armenian young lady in Paris only four or five years ago about Armenian writing, especially poetry, and this woman had a very thick body, very thick legs and ankles, and was having an affair with a married Frenchman of fifty to her thirty, and her father was angry at her, and told me to try to convince her to end that stupid affair and marry an Armenian, but of course I never did any such thing, although I did ask her, since she seemed to have such positive opinions of every poet of Armenia, to tell me about your poetry, and Hrachia I must tell you what she said because you are no longer a naive young man, you are a big drinking heavy hearty man who has lived the better part of his life, she said, Oh, he is a writer of nice cuddly poems—cuddly, for Christ's sake. And I was annoyed, because if ever there was a female whose body was totally beyond being cuddly, who couldn't be cuddled by anybody at all, it was this silly woman, so I told her that she was thinking of perhaps one of your love lyrics which was tender deliberately, so quickly she began to recite such a poem, and she made the thing sound cuddly, she gave a performance, she demonstrated the truth of her theory, which I considered a damned false truth, she mocked and belittled a poet of the people, and I made up my mind to avoid that stupid woman and never permit myself to be where I might be unable to avoid her—in short, never to visit her father's tailor shop again. And I thank Christ that so far I have had great good luck. Perhaps there was an element of truth in her theory, but there is a far greater element of untruth. She simply wanted to ridicule simple love between a man and a woman to justify somewhat her own sloppy stupid affair with a sneak. I hope you are not hurt by this anecdote.

HRACHIA. Oh, no, no, this is old stuff for me, but you are right, the poem is a people's poem. It is indeed gentle, but not cuddly.

BITLIS. Excuse me. I've come back. Has anybody seen my keys? I was at the Metro station for the long ride home when I discovered that I don't have my keys. Arpik, please forgive me. I am sorry about this second intrusion. You are quite right. My memoirs are silly. Have you seen my keys? Who needs to know what I remember in the Tsapergor Tagh of Bitlis seventy or more years ago? I could go home and hope to climb in safely through a window, but who really needs to know that in my father's eyes I saw nothing but anger and sorrow one day after another because there was no hope for us, and yet what could we do? We did not have the money with which to run away. I always keep my keys in this pocket, but at the Metro station I found it empty, absolutely empty, and somebody told me just last year that our cemetery on the hillside going up to Tsapergor, the Turks have destroyed, and my father's stone has been taken away for street paving, and I said to myself, better go back to Arpik's, you must have left the keys there somewhere when you brought from your jacket pocket the manuscript of your memoirs, surely you have my keys, do you not?

ARPIK. Oh, for heaven's sake, my dear friend, Dikran Boshbazmanian, please give me the manuscript of your memoirs of Bitlis, I will publish them, but it is too late for tomorrow's issue, I will get them into the issue for the day after tomorrow, and now that you are back, sit down, please, I am sure your keys will turn up somehow, and if they don't have no care, I will drive with Zohrab to your house, and he will climb through the window and let you in. Give me the manuscript, please.

BITLIS. No, no, really, I feel terrible losing face and pride this way. You do not want my memoirs, so why should I give you my manuscript?

ARPIK. I want your memoirs. *Haratch* needs your memoirs. There are not many more of you older boys with memoirs of Van, Moush, Sassoun, Kars, Ardahan, Erzeroum, Dikranagert, and all of the other great cities of our country. I made a mistake in not letting you know that your memoirs are the very thing *Haratch* needs, for that is the simple truth, as I am sure our other friends here will agree, will you not?

HRACHIA.   I certainly do.

KHACHIG.   Of course, of course, and if any of us had any sense we
would sit down with you one hour a day for the next year or two
and put on magnetophone tape your remarks about your life in Bitlis.
There is a whole big project of that kind going on all over America,
you know, and so far the results are amazing. Of course we agree
with Arpik that your memoirs must appear in *Haratch*.

BITLIS.   You may remove anything from this manuscript, Arpik, that
you believe ought to be removed. I refer to an Armenian informer,
and it has troubled me that he was an Armenian, and that he did
it for money, but not nearly enough money, and he was shot like
a dog, after a trial in our church just at the edge of our cemetery,
which is now a cattle barn, according to a traveler to Bitlis a few
years ago, and in the tower there are many pigeons and their
droppings are everywhere. Take out the part perhaps about poor
Anoushavan Vashpazian, poor, poor fellow, my father came home
from the meeting and said, They shot him like a dog, he did not
complain, but the way he looked at them, I will never forget it.
Money, the need of money, does terrible things to all of us, is that
not so?

HRACHIA.   Down through the ages it has made fools of all of us, and
I lift my glass to the memory of the informer. What did you say
his name was?

BITLIS.   Anoushavan Vashpazian.

HRACHIA.   Yes, well what made you remember his name, for God's
sake?

BITLIS.   What my father said about his silence, and his eyes.

HRACHIA.   When your manuscript is published in *Haratch* day after
tomorrow I want to read it very carefully. As for your keys, what's
that, what's that?

BITLIS.   Ah, yes, these are my keys, I have been holding them ever
since I left here, and I didn't know it, but we are strange are we
not all of us who belong to the human race. Why was I clutching
my keys and yet did not know that I was doing so? But please, please
do me the honor of cutting out any part of my manuscript that you
believe does not do honor to the Armenian people. Is it necessary,
I am saying, to speak of poor Anoushavan Vashpazian at all? Why
not let the dear sad man lie in his disgrace where he has been all
these terrible years.

ARPIK. I will see, I will see.

HRACHIA. Dear friend from Bitlis, son of the shoemaker, here is your own Saroyan, whose people went from Bitlis to Fresno, and you must know by now, since he has been publishing books for almost fifty years, he writes and writes and writes, all the time. Saroyan, tell this old writer, your friend, and tell me, also your friend, and tell Arpik, and Khachig, and Sylvia, and Zohrab, and the world, not just the world of Armenians, but the world of everybody, what are you writing now. I know from looking at you that you are writing and writing and writing. You have told me so yourself, both in Fresno when I visited your house and again in Erevan when we sat and ate and drank. But now, now, Saroyan, what are you writing?

KHACHIG. And why?

SAROYAN. Yes, that is the best part of that question. Why? Well, I will tell you why. In order to avoid dying, that's why. And that is why all of us do whatever it is that we do. That is why Hrachia is drinking that whiskey. And how good it is not to die, just to drink whiskey and have everything that is too much for us blur and fade and be forgotten.

HRACHIA. Never mind why, we know why, but what are you writing and writing and writing, now, Saroyan? Tell this good old man. Arpik is going to publish your latest memories of childhood in the next issue of *Haratch*, Arpik is a very great Armenian, and there is one thing about her that I am surprised nobody seems to have noticed, except me. And I notice this thing every time I see her. I marvel at it. What are you writing, Saroyan?

SAROYAN. Well, you know that like my good friend from Bitlis I write only memoirs, only autobiography, because it is my belief that only in this kind of straightforward writing can we reach the reader, and there is really no excuse for writing except to reach the reader, no matter who he is, and that means everything I write is like an open letter to anybody who is able to read. And so, you are quite right, Hrachia, I am writing and writing.

KHACHIG. But why? You have said it is in order not to die, but that is not enough. Why? Why do you not take your fortune and go out and spend it all on yourself and your family and friends and yes, even young girls, there are many who would feel very happy to have your intimate friendship, nothing is more appealing to some pretty girls than a famous man, no matter how old he is—Sylvia says she finds you very attractive. Why do you write instead of forgetting the hard work of it, on and on, and go out and do nothing but spend money and enjoy life?

HRACHIA.   Why do you ask such really foolish questions, Khachig?

SAROYAN.   No, no, Hrachia, it is not a foolish question. I like it, and I have given the matter great thought, prolonged thought, over many years, and again I am obliged to make the only answer I believe is true: it is not possible for me to celebrate success, for I do not believe I am a success, I have never celebrated any achievement. I have no wish to be a young man again, although sometimes I have pangs of longing for that terrible time which years later the soul distorts and pretends was a great time. Youth is the most terrible time of all. I do not want to fall in love in the way of youth. I have always been in love in the way of age and experience, as I am right now—with everybody, especially the ugly, the poor, the rejected, the deprived, the unhappy, the lonely, the unfortunate, the sick, the insane, and all of the other disasters of the human race—and the reason I love them all is that through such love I am able to cherish more deeply our everlasting and inexhaustible health, our intelligence, our handsomeness, the beauty of our women not just in body alone but in spirit. If I were to go out and celebrate, what would it be that I would be celebrating? Meaninglessness? Not for myself alone, but for all of us, for the whole human race, for all of its history, for nature itself? I have acquired through hard steadfast faith and work a certain order of private meaning, but it would be impossible for me to go and celebrate that very special and limited and useless achievement. What is it Hrachia that you have noticed about our beloved Arpik?

HRACHIA.   Her feet. They're very small. Very narrow. They are like a pair of doves, almost. It is a wonderful thing to behold every time I see Arpik. Her feet are two love birds. How proud Schavarch your father must be that his little girl has not permitted his paper *Haratch* to die.

ARPIK.   I expected you to notice my intelligence and my charity, Hrachia.

HRACHIA.   No, your feet.

ARPIK.   I have had in mind for several years devoting one issue a month to strictly literary matters. The first Sunday of each month. Does this idea appeal to you? Yes, I do mean you. Does it?

BITLIS. I am not a literary writer, as you know. But if you have decided that you want such an issue every month, I am sure it is a very sensible idea. I have poems, I write a least one poem a week, but I have never brought them to you, because I have read the poems you have published and they are so much better than my poems. Zulal here had such a poem in yesterday's issue. Oh, that was so wise, Zulal, so really right.

ZULAL. When I die, wherever it may be, whenever it must be, I have no request to make of Armenia, or of any Armenian. I shall not ask that I must be buried at the foot of Ararat, or along the banks of the Euphrates, I shall die, I shall be dead, it is not necessary for me to give heroic instructions to the rest of the family about what to do with me.

ARPIK. This is not what you said in your poem, dear heart Zulal.

ZULAL. What did I say?

ARPIK. You said, Know this, Armenia, my place waits for me at the top of Ararat. And what was the other line? I have no memory for poetry.

BITLIS. My soul like a bird shall be on its way there before I am cold. Those are words, Zulal, they are poetic words. I write only peoples' words.

ZULAL. It comes to the same thing, and let us ask ourselves why do we hold fast to Ararat, why does Ararat mean so much to Armenians and so little to Turks, for Ararat is part of the geography of Turkey, and Armenians are only able to see it just across the border, beyond the plains of October.

SAROYAN. Well, if we are going to ask rhetorical questions, Zulal, old friend, new friend, let us begin at the beginning, shall we, as my old acquaintance Leopold Stokowski used to say, after asking the most simple question or after making the most simple remark, such as, Well, let us now decide on where we shall go for lunch, or if we shall fix our own lunch and have it here, shall we? And please overlook this unnecessary preamble about poor old Stokowski, he died last year at the age of ninety-nine, wasn't it? My question is this. What is an Armenian? Who is an Armenian?

ZULAL. No, why is an Armenian? Where is an Armenian? When is an Armenian? And the answer is this: An Armenian is a Turk who says I am an Armenian. It is a decision open to all people, and only Armenians have ever wanted to be Armenians, everybody else has not made a decision but has gone right on being whatever it was he believed he was, anyhow. You have got to choose to be an Armenian, you have got to want to be an Armenian, and here we are seven or eight Armenians asking and answering questions, and moving ourselves steadily toward a destination, that does not exist. About flying to the top of Ararat at death, well, don't we know that I shall do no such thing, and that only a poet not yet fifty years old would want to say such a thing.

BITLIS.   I would want to, and I am well along into time, and nearer to the end than anybody else here, and I know that when I die I shall somehow reach Ararat, but I don't know how I shall get there. Perhaps I shall walk, from Tsapergor Tagh, we used to walk from Bitlis to Van, to Moush, to Sassoun, you know. I suppose that when I die I shall continue to move as I always have. Well, Arpik, and all, please know how deeply happy you have made me, I have found my keys, and so I will say goodbye.

HRACHIA.   No, no, you must stay as long as we are together this way, and furthermore you must accept a glass of whiskey from our good American colleague Khachig, and when that bottle is empty, look here, here is much money, French money, please go and bring another bottle.

ARPIK.   I have bottles of whiskey, gin, vodka, arak, brandy, so you need not spend your money, Hrachia.

HRACHIA.   You have small feet, Arpik, the feet of a girl I know Kuchak would write a poem about. How can you stand upon doves instead of feet, Armenian girl, Kuchak would have written.

ZULAL.   I don't think so. Although he loved the girls, it was not their feet that he noticed, and we all know what it was that he did notice, and we know how right he was. But Kuchak didn't tell us anything about himself except that he loved the girls.

HRACHIA.   He was a real Armenian.

KHACHIG.   Let us drink to Kuchak's girls with their white bosoms, then...I have a friend who is an Assyrian, but he doesn't speak that language, he speaks Armenian, and of course English, and he is learning Russian because he believes it will be a good thing to read Tchekhov untranslated. Well, my question is this: is this friend of mine an Assyrian, actually? In view of the fact that there has been no geographical Assyria in centuries. He does not even speak the language, he is studying Russian and not Assyrian, he speaks

Armenian as his family language because his people have always been close to the Armenians, and he looks as Armenian as many or even most Armenians look Assyrian. I mean, what about us? Not just the few of us here in the editorial office of *Haratch*. I mean, Armenians everywhere. Are we Armenians, or are we indeed something else?

HRACHIA. My boy, I am astonished by your question. I thought you must be very perceptive and intelligent, having gone to American universities, and being a teacher in one. Are we Armenians? If you mean, is there a future for Armenians in the Dispersion, there is some merit to your question, for if we are realistic and not dreamers, we must accept the probability that in a predictable amount of time the Armenians in the Dispersion will cease to be Armenians. It will take a century, it may take two centuries, but the probability is very strong, and we must in turn understand this probability and accept it, or reject it.

ZOHRAB.   So what if we do reject it? How does that help us? I have rejected it all my life, but here I am living in the suburbs of Paris, my wife is Armenian, we have no children, we have not even adopted an Armenian orphan or two, and all I think about is that when I die, that will be the end of my family, and I will be buried in a strange cemetery, and it will mean nothing, absolutely nothing. So what good is it that I reject these simple unavoidable facts.

HRACHIA.   My friend, go to Armenia, go and die there, and let your bones join the rocks of our beautiful Armenia. That's how. And that is the way all Armenians in the Dispersion are free to reject the inevitable disappearance of themselves far from home. Go home, and every day somebody is doing that, and not just the angry people who thirty or forty years ago left America and went home, and then began to cry because life was so different in Armenia, and most of them finally went back to Rhode Island, and Connecticut, and Massachusetts, and New York. We all learned a lot from that chapter of Armenian history. A return to Armenia cannot be based upon hatred for America, for instance, it has got to be something better than that. It cannot be an outburst of emotionalism, of fantasy, of the expectation of fulfillment of the false dreams of the heart. Anybody who returns to Armenia must know that he is sacrificing things that are painful to sacrifice, he must know that housing in Armenia is going to be nothing at all like what he knew in France, for instance. He must know that taking an evening walk in Armenia is not going to be like taking a drive across America in a Cadillac. But he will discover that in walking in Erevan he is walking in Armenia, in his own country, through his own ancient experience, and that he is not racing across a whole continent looking for himself. We are as good as finished in the Dispersion, that's true, but we are only just beginning to be fully ourselves in Armenia, yes, Soviet Armenia, which I know many of us all over the world believe is a terrible dictatorship and something like a terrible misfortune. Don't believe it, Khachig. Just believe that yes, we are lost forever in the Dispersion, and no, we are not finished as a people with a proud history, a great culture, a magnificent present, and the means to preserve our beautiful past, with all of its failures, and to move along fruitfully into our even more beautiful future. By God, I said it, and I know it is not just this whiskey, although you may pour just a drop more in this glass, and then I will stop. I like to drink but nobody has ever seen me drunk.

ARPIK.   Have you seen yourself drunk, Hrachia?

HRACHIA.   Yes, just now, but you cannot, any of you, truthfully say that you saw me drunk, can you? And who disagrees with me? Who? Who?

ARPIK.   Who can disagree with the sun and the moon and the stars?

HRACHIA.   Arpik, you stand on doves, not feet. You are a bird.

STEPAN.   Ah ha, so here you have all gathered, have you? Well, how fortunate I am to have come at such a time.

ARPIK.   Come in, come in, I won't introduce anybody at all, and everybody knows you are a bishop at our church on Rue Jean Goujon—Bishop Stepan. Khachig pour the bishop a drink.

STEPAN.   Half, then, Khachig, and my dear countrymen, I do not see a foreign face here, and that makes me very happy.

ZOHRAB.   Forget the religious talk, Stepan. We are talking about life.

STEPAN.   Zohrab, my old old childhood friend, I am so glad God has spared you from the minds and knives of the doctors—you look very well, skinny perhaps, but it seems to suit you. We are getting old, old friend.

ZOHRAB.   There are others here who are far older than we are, skinnier, and in any case you are fat. You are fat. Church people eat too much. They have insatiable appetites. What stories we have all heard about them.

STEPAN.   Yes, yes, and so have we, of the church, and if the stories are not lies, they are not the truth either. Continue, continue, please, go right on, I am off-duty, I am walking for the good of my soul which I sometimes think must be pagan, or also pagan, after it is Christian, for I need to be alone, far from the church, far from the very memory of prayer and supplication, but I thought as I walked, is this not near *Haratch*, then let me go there and perhaps I will find Arpik still at her desk, and one or two others, and we will visit and talk, but I never expected to find such a fascinating crowd as this, and I must ask quickly, Who here is not Christian? Who? Anybody? Then, it is I alone who is the pagan. And I am a bishop in the Church and I wear the robes and carry the staff, and all the while deep in my heart I am a pagan, I don't believe at all.

HRACHIA.   If a man of the church is not a pagan he does not belong in the church. If he does not know he is a pagan, he needs further schooling and perhaps a few years in the marketplace among the great trials and tribulations of the poor, scrounging one another for a small profit, enough for the day's bread. The pagan prays, Give us this day our daily wine. Is Vasken also a pagan, then?

STEPAN.   Ah, do not tempt me, I do not wish to speak for our great Vehapar, Vasken the First, for if you have met him, as I am sure many here have, each of you must answer for himself about that good man. I cannot. Let us speak about *Haratch*, our only daily paper in Europe.

KHACHIG.   There are two in Istanbul—*Marmara* and *Zhamanak*.

STEPAN.   Istanbul is in Asia, not Europe. Arpik, you must be admired again, for only this morning I read your letter to our beloved Antranik. It was inspired, and your Armenian is so much more appealing than the Armenian of our good friends in Erevan.

ARPIK.   We were speaking about that a moment ago, but you are a man of Erevan, you were educated in Etchmiadzin, why do you find fault with the Armenian that is written and spoken in Soviet Armenia.

STEPAN.   I do not find fault, I simply say that your Armenian appeals to me more. And the things you wrote in your letter to Antranik, they were beautiful things, Arpik. Tears came to my eyes.

ARPIK.   Tears come to your eyes easily.

HRACHIA.   And to mine, because if somebody writes well, it is necessary for me to show my silent secret appreciation with a few tears, and then my jealousy comes raging out of a cage like a tiger and I say, How dare she write better than I write? That's not fair, I am the writer whose writing should bring tears to all Armenian eyes. But Arpik you told our great General Antranik a few things that needed to be told.

KHACHIG. And what did Antranik reply, Arpik? What did he say? Did he say, What dreamers you are, all of you. I have been dead more than fifty years? Have you not found a new hero, for the love of God? While I was alive, between the political parties you tore me to pieces and you made my life an agony. Well, you must know that I admire Antranik as much as any of you, but the poor man must have passed his last years in terrible loneliness—the dangers and treacheries of war made sense to him. Peace was only a time of talk, not action, and he was not much of a talker. In fact I have heard that he really was not a talker at all. So now we are all great talkers. Here's to us, then.

SAROYAN. Do you like being an Armenian?

STEPAN. Who?

SAROYAN. All of you, and yet only you asked, so how and why did that happen? Is it possible that you have given that question a good deal of thought, especially lately. I mean, how did it happen that none of you asked that question? Only he asked it.

ARPIK. It is a foolish question, perhaps that's way.

SAROYAN. Where you surprised to hear it?

ZOHRAB. Not from you, for you do ask sudden questions, and I am used to it.

SAROYAN. Hrachia, you are the only one here from Soviet Armenia. Why didn't you ask that question? Who?

HRACHIA. How can you say I am the only one here from Soviet Armenia? Stepan was born near Etchmiadzin, he was schooled there, he is given assignments all around the world from Etchmiadzin, he has already served our church in Detroit, Teheran, Buenos Aires, and several other places. He alone asked because he is alert and is quick to respond. Is that so, then, Stepan?

STEPAN. We are standing here, drinking, talking, and being Armenians, and Saroyan throws out a wild question, Do you like being an Armenian? And I ask Who, who is he asking? So this is the center of a big Armenian discussion and dispute. Do you like being an Armenian? Do you like being Saroyan? Do you like being anybody? Do you like *gahdah*?

SAROYAN. Well, it happens that at our house in Fresno *gahdah* was only infrequently put upon the tables, we preferred plain *bagharch*, as I still do, but do you know, there are almost no women left in Fresno who know how to make the dough and bake either the famous *lahvash*, or flat bread, or the *bagharch*, which some liken to *peda*, although there is only a similarity of shape. Yes, I like *gahdah*, or Armenian plain cake, but let me ask again, Do you like being an Armenian?

SYLVIA. Let me perhaps not keep my place as an Armenian young lady among a group of Armenian young and old men, and let me reply by saying that although years ago I rather disliked being Armenian because it seemed to make trouble for me at school and out in society, as the saying goes, more and more as I mature I find that I like being Armenian.

SAROYAN. I thank you, Sylvia. Why do you like being an Armenian, though?

SYLVIA. We must like what we are, or we shall surely make ourselves very unhappy and surely also very sick. Why should I not like being an Armenian?

SAROYAN. We lost all our wars, and according to Michael J. Arlen in *Passage to Ararat* the truth has given us a terrible inferiority complex, and he also put forward the theory that we refuse to forget the crime of genocide inflicted upon us by Turkey because we have profound self-hatred, and don't know what else to do to somehow deliver ourselves from this destructive condition. We are losers and we hate ourselves for not being winners.

HRACHIA. This is nonsense. He wrote a good book, I met him when he came to Armenia, he is a very fine young fellow, and a good writer, but his theory is false. We do not forget the massacres because in not forgetting we rejoice in our survival against terrible odds. Communism does not encourage rivalry among peoples, but I invite everybody here to compare the achievements in fifty years of Soviet Armenia with the achievements during the same time of Turkey. What is it that the Turks have done with their ownership of our lands and cities, and with the banishment of our people, and with the continuing animosity toward all Armenian institutions and peoples—the few that remain in Istanbul and Ankara, Izmir and Erzeroum. I have heard of nothing. Certainly nothing of any interest to the world, to people everywhere. We have sent out through Aram

Khatchatourian our music. Through Martiros Sarian our painting.
Through Victor Hampartzoumian our science. And many many
others. What about the Turks? Do they like being Turks? Yes of
course they do. But only because nature demands that of all of us.
And if anybody here doesn't like being an Armenian—don't worry
about it, nature also demands that of all of us. When I am a fool,
I don't like being an Armenian, because I am an Armenian fool,
and that makes hard work for other Armenians to do, to balance
my folly.

BITLIS.　I never believed the day would come when I would be in the
editorial office of *Haratch* at the same time with so many great
Armenians. This is an honor I shall never, never forget.

ARPIK.　Perhaps you will include it, then, in your memoirs.

BITLIS.　When? Who can live long enough to remember all of his
great experiences. I am still in Bitlis. I have not even reached
Erzeroum on the way to Trabizond and Samsun and Bolis and Athens
and Genoa and Marseilles and I have so much to remember, but
nothing more exciting more pleasant than this gathering together
of great Armenians.

KHACHIG.　Well, perhaps you could use this in a special memoir and
not wait until you had caught up with everything else, first. That
also is sometimes done. An interlude, something extra, a special,
as it were. What would you say? How would you remember yourself
here at this moment?

BITLIS.　I would forget myself, I would remember you with the bottle,
like some kind of treasure of the church or of the editorial office,
and I would remember the talk and the listening, and now I have
said enough, I want to listen, I do not want to talk, please forgive
me I was overcome by your words, all of you. How exciting it is
to be Armenian. I would not trade that truth for anything in the
whole world.

ARPIK.　Please put some whiskey into his glass, Khachig, he has never
spoken this way at all before.

BITLIS.　No, no, it is not the whiskey and I do not want any more,
just enough to suit the spirit of this occasion, that is all. Please go
on, please let me just stand here and listen.

ARPIK.　Well, at least sit down.

SYLVIA.　Here, please, I am tired of sitting.

BITLIS. Oh, Armenian maid, how sweet you are, but do you know, until Arpik asked me to sit down I did not even know that I was standing and have been standing for so long. Either I am stronger than I know, or the excitement of this Armenian event has made me forget myself entirely. As Arpik says I do not speak as I have spoken. What did I say? My memory fails me. I really don't know what I said, what I am saying. Perhaps I am dying.

ARPIK. Oh, no, that is all I need—for you to die here. My good old friend, please keep yourself alive, please don't die. Just sit and go right on looking at the face of every speaker and go on listening so eagerly to every word he says.

BITLIS. Thank you, as you know, I am from Bitlis. My father was a shoemaker, and my mother was the beloved daughter of a shoemaker.

ARPIK. Yes, it is this new memoir which I shall publish with a great deal of pride and pleasure in the next issue of *Haratch*.

ZOHRAB. I was told that frequently a man of Bitlis would walk all the way to my city, Moush. Did you ever do that?

ARPIK. Zohrab, please let the man from Bitlis rest a moment or two.

ZOHRAB. Well, of course, of course, Arpik, so let me say this, then: only last year, before I had the heart attack, I walked down from the Opera to Issy-les-Moulineaux where I visited the church. I was only on my feet about three hours, and that night I felt the strain of it so sharply I could barely sleep. Well, I have heard that a walk from Bitlis to Moush began at daybreak and ended at dusk, a matter of not three hours but of perhaps thirteen or fourteen, but I never took that walk, and so I can't be sure.

ARPIK. Zohrab, I want to ask Khachig who teaches English and American literature at a fine college in Connecticut—would you teach at a college in Frezzzno? I mean there are Armenians who do not like Frezzzno. One of them was in this very office one day, and he made a big point of correcting me. He said, No, Madame, I am not from Frezzzno, I am from Pasadena. Well, what is it about Pasadena that is so much better than Frezzzno?

SAROYAN. I think what he meant was that he was a man of some wealth and perhaps some culture, especially in connection with rugs, for there are more rug dealers in Pasadena than even in New York, while in Fresno there is not one, and if you want such a rug you must find a private party that has one he is willing to sell or you must go to San Francisco. Pasadena is far far superior to Frezzzno, as the man told you. Didn't you notice?

ARPIK. No, I don't believe I did. Hrachia, please wake up. Why are you nodding your head, soon you will be snoring.

HRACHIA. It is because I am home, I am in Armenia in this place...Why, tell me, my friend William, why did you ask, a moment ago, Do you like being an Armenian? And the reason I ask is that they say every question we ask others is a question we have already asked ourselves, and if that is so, I want to hear about it. Have you perhaps found it really difficult to be an Armenian? Have you disliked being an Armenian yourself?

SAROYAN. Yes, of course. How could I possibly not dislike being not just an Armenian, but myself? That is where it all begins of course, as we all know. In the self, which is essentially universal, I should think, and if anything, anti-nationality, anti-classification, anti-limitation of any order. Not that the self is anarchistic, quite the contrary, it is terribly rigid in its formalism, but this rigidity does not in the slightest degree inhibit or tend to halt the enormous potentiality of the self for all truth, reality, character, meaning, intelligence, ability, grace, and all of the other things that are the common property of the human race—at its best.

KHACHIG. And what about the human race at its worst?

SAROYAN. The worst of the human race is so much a part of the best that while it is convenient in talk and in writing to make the differentiation the fact is that the worst and the best are the same. But you are right to ask, because I did say the human race at its best. The worst that the human race has done is still not altogether removed from a dimension of both innocence and insignificance, comparatively.

KHACHIG. The massacres were innocent and insignificant? Are you sure?

SAROYAN. How could I be sure? How could you? How could truth? How could God? But I do believe that if we consider the massacres fully and in detail we will probably discover that they were both innocent and insignificant. Who is it that suffers the greatest loss in a massacre, those who are massacred, or those who massacre them? I urge you not to answer instantly, I urge you to think. And I urge you to take into account that if there has ever been a massacre which did indeed wipe out a whole people, I do not know of it, and the survivors of an attempted genocide, let us think about them a moment, and let us at least suspect that what happens to them is far more usable than what happens to the survivors of those who attempted the Genocide—for one by little one, human beings with their truths and secrets die, and their children take their places: if the killers deny that they killed, and they slowly die, their children are burdened with a variety of diseases or self-deceptions or paralyzing unconfessed truths, while the children of the survivors, the sons and daughters, so to put it, of the murdered and massacred, even the sons and daughters of boys and girls who did not live long enough to become mothers and fathers, are endowed from these truths, and the survival of themselves in spite of the terrible martyrdom of their parents, with great human qualities which must compel in the entire family a profound strengthening of the durability that is in all human beings, and must also compel greater wit and compassion, creativity and control, and all of the other qualities that are the human race's glory, of all branches of it. No, I am not sure the massacres were innocent and insignificant, but I think they must have been, or something useful to the whole human race would have come into the entire Turkish people as a consequence of the massacres, and so far there does not appear to be any evidence of that.

SYLVIA. Is this a suggestion perhaps that the Armenians have mourned their martyrs long enough, as Michael Arlen seems to have said in one way or another in *Passage to Ararat*?

SAROYAN. No, I don't believe so. If there is an element of sorry sameness to our racial grief, let it be so, for there are other elements in it, also, and memory does not go on forever, let us please remember: we have kids all over the world who are the children of the children of the children of the children who were massacred and never lived to have children of their own, if you can follow what I am saying, and these children seem to know that it is right for them not to forget—until it can't be helped, and the forgetting happens by itself, perhaps out of the increasing of the whole family into largeness, instead of a few million, many million, and great power, even to the point of being equal to the perpetrating of massacre upon others—but don't be unhappy and read into this remark more than what I am saying, which is that we are all of us the same, but differently of course.

COP.   Please excuse me, but is anybody here the owner of the red Fiat out front? It is being visited by two small boys and two small girls who insist the automobile belongs to their father.

ARPIK.   Perhaps it does.

COP.   They are not brothers and sisters, I'm afraid.

KHACHIG.   Couldn't they possibly be?

COP.   One is black, one is yellow, one is red, and the smallest boy seems to be French.

SYLVIA.   Perhaps they have a common mother. That happens in every big city, even in Pasadena.

COP.   Then, nobody here is the owner of the automobile?

ARPIK.   I think not, but let me go with you and see the boys and girls.

SAROYAN.   What's that all about?

HRACHIA.   Saroyan, you amaze me, you have lived in Paris twenty years but still you don't understand French, and I come here only now and then for a few days and I seem to understand everything.

SAROYAN.   I'm deaf, or at any rate half-deaf, I swear I don't hear anything anybody says, but when somebody speaks English or Armenian I understand everything partly from the little I do hear, partly from the voice itself and the style of speech, and partly from memory. Just now I believe I understood every word you said excepting perhaps the very first part, after you said my name. What did you say, then?

HRACHIA.   I said I don't understand.

SAROYAN.   Arpik, are they brothers and sisters, the four of them?

ARPIK.   They are now six, three boys and three girls, and they are kids of the neighborhood. They are doing no real harm, they are only pretending to be rich and the owners of a red Fiat with leather upholstery.

SAROYAN.   Why did the cop feel he must come in here about the matter?

ARPIK.   The car is parked directly out front. And of course he is a Paris cop and he enjoys making contact with the people of this neighborhood.

SAROYAN.   Shall we bring the children in, then? Perhaps one of them is an Armenian.

ARPIK.   I don't think so, although one boy might be an Arab, and one girl might be Jewish, and they appear to be devoted to one another, the girl eight or nine and the boy eleven or twelve.

SAROYAN. Khachig, perhaps you ought to go out there and if one of the boys or girls is Armenian, bring him or her into this room, so that we can get the viewpoint of our very youngest people about being Armenian.

ARPIK. Ah, no, Saroyan, and by now that little congregation has been dispersed. I handed out to each little hand one franc each, and they have gone to buy sweets down the street.

SAROYAN. Why did you hand them one franc? Do you do that sort of thing as part of your character, or what?

ARPIK. Yes, I think we can say that. Yes, I like to hand out small coins to small hands, or large coins to the larger hands of older people.

SAROYAN. Do they hold their hands out to you?

ARPIK. Almost never. But I know who needs a coin and who doesn't. The beggar with the hand held out never needs a coin. He is quite rich, or she owns the building in which you have your apartment. Isn't it so in America?

SAROYAN. It is said to be so, but I have never believed it. What sort of kids were they?

ARPIK. Kids of the street, of the neighborhood, Paris kids, international kids. They are wise in the way of the world, but they have their pride, and while they will readily accept a coin they would never, never ask for one—even in a very real emergency of some kind.

SAROYAN. You sound as if you might be the mother of the six kids.

ARPIK. Well, it doesn't take any women very long to sound like the mother of all kids if she has none of her own, I suppose. Every issue of this paper *Haratch* is a new child, I suppose.

KHACHIG. But you have favorites, of course.

ARPIK. Yes, perhaps I do, but not really. I like them all, especially those issues that seem altogether ordinary, I don't know why.

SAROYAN. Love has got to cherish the least with the most, that's why.

ACT THREE

ZULAL. I've said it many times. You can have Byron and Shelley, give me Keats.

ARPIK. Dear heart, what are you talking about? Where have you been?

ZULAL. I am translating a poem by Keats, from English into Armenian, even though my translation is from French into Armenian, I have been right here at the edge of this table. Keats is gentle, he is kind to all of us.

HRACHIA. I like all three, they were English but they were wild and each of them died young, after a busy life, especially Byron. He studied Armenian, you know, with the Mekhitarists on the Island of San Lazzaro.

ZULAL. It was a purely therapeutic measure when he was falling to pieces and was having an affair with an old Venetian's young and passionate titled lady. Trying to learn Armenian permitted him to rest a moment. He was moving steadily towards insanity or death, and he was most fortunate that he took ill at Missalonghi and quickly died, perhaps just in time to avoid running amuck. I like him, but I like Keats better.

BITLIS. Who? Who is it studied Armenian? Why?

ARPIK. Byron, Lord Byron.

BITLIS. The name is familiar, but I don't seem to know it.

ZULAL. Keats had a heart, Byron had a heart, too, but it was not a heart of the heart itself, or the soul, it was a heart of the mind, or intelligence, and he could be very swift and short with people whose hearts were of the heart itself. He drove some of his own people mad, almost, and certainly hurried them to their graves.

ARPIK. But they say all such considerations are besides the point if his poetry is good.

ZULAL. No, no, not good, great. In order for a poet to be an assassin his poetry must be great. At least that, but even then there are those who do not accept his poetry at all, because he himself was such an assassin.

KHACHIG. Who do we have like Byron, then?

ZULAL. Well, we are all a little like him who write poems, or even who only read them. Everybody fails to avoid the equivalent of the inflicting of pain or even death upon others, especially those nearest and dearest to him, at some time or another. It happens, it seems to be part of our fate, if you happen to believe in fate, or the forehead-writing.

KHACHIG. Well, I don't disbelieve in forehead-writing, perhaps because the old women of my family have said my own forehead-writing is excellent, I am destined to live a good life, all the way. But at the same time I also believe that it is for me to decide how good my good life is to be.

SYLVIA. How good should a good life be, then?

KHACHIG. Well, good enough not to make a fool of a man, I suppose.

SYLVIA. Why would living a good life, or a good good life, make a fool of a man, pray tell?

KHACHIG. Very well, I will pray tell. By making him intolerant of the bad life lived by people whose forehead-writing was quite poor, and on top of that who were altogether without the required force and energy of mind and spirit to decide for themselves how to live the good life.

SYLVIA. Well, I don't know. Why should a superior man want to look down at an inferior man? I mean, the most superior man is also inferior to somebody, and if not, he is certainly not nearly as superior as he might be had he just had a little more force and will, or as he might be by the grace of God.

BITLIS. We have our Armenian God to thank again and again for our good fortune in being Armenians, for it we had not been, then of course we would have disappeared from the face of the earth long ago when so many other people in that part of the world disappeared. I read about this in our beloved Samuelian's many excellent and wise pieces published in *Haratch* and now the great man is dead, how many days is it, Arpik?

ARPIK. He died three or four years ago.

BITLIS. What a loss, and the bookshop, is it still there, on Monsieur-le-Prince? For even a bookshop full of books can disappear from the face of the earth, God help us all who are Armenians. Is the bookshop gone?

ARPIK. No, his son and his daughter are in charge.

BITLIS. Thank God, then. Do they write as their father wrote?

ARPIK. No, they don't. At least not so far.

BITLIS. Some day, some day, then, perhaps they will. They must, Armenia must go on.

HRACHIA. I want to make an announcement. I think we are the luckiest people in the world. I mean this, I really think that is the simple truth.

ZOHRAB. What are you talking about? You are at least twice as fat as you ought to be. You will be dead suddenly from a heart attack, long before even I will be, and I know I haven't got very long, certainly not forever, which is what I believed I had before I had the heart attack which I am not sure might just as well have taken me out of life and set me down in total forgetfulness. I mean, is this being alive? This? Really. I am not who I am any more. Is it desirable for a man not to be who he is? So what are you talking about, my old friend. How many easy walks you and I have taken in our beloved Erevan over the years, and now you can't walk for the fat on your frame, and I can't for being a virtual prisoner of the defective heart, mended and patched with veins from my own ankle and foot. What for? So that I can stand and walk feebly, like some kind of invalid. It is a kind of shamelessness the way I insist that even this is something, and better than nothing. Why do you say we are the luckiest people in the world? You're fat and I'm an invalid.

HRACHIA. Even so, even so, brother Zohrab of Moush, do not despair, you may be an invalid in body but you are free and strong in spirit, or how would you have made the vigorous protestation I was just now astonished and delighted to hear—for the truth is the truth and there is no substitute for it at all, certainly no lie or no grouping of lies can compare with the simple truth.

KHACHIG. Yes, yes, but we are all dying to hear why you think we are the luckiest people in the world, especially those of us here who are not much past the age of thirty, so why, why are we so lucky?

SYLVIA. He means himself and myself—not yet past the age of thirty, but look here, Khachig, there is nobody here who is really very much past thirty, and indeed very much past eighteen, for as we know the limits of intelligence are reached well before that age, after which only experience may be said to be added to the material upon which intelligence is presumed to work. I don't have to be told why we are the luckiest people in the world. I know.

KHACHIG. You do? Why? I mean, don't invent suddenly, tell what you have already told in your tone of voice, and don't fall silent and become ashamed. This is the family and so we will not think less of you. Why?

SYLVIA. Because we are lovers. We love life. We love art. We love being alive. We love the mystery of it. And I love you.

KHACHIG. That's the part I thought I heard in your tone of voice, and I mean hushed with joy, and am obliged now to ask everybody here to forgive us, for we also are eighteen years old, or less, and in love. Move along, then, Hrachia, and tell us why—if you really know.

BITLIS. What did he say? I didn't quite hear him. What did she say?

ARPIK. These young people are sweethearts, it would seem, as if any of us had not noticed, but for God's sake don't go soft and silly and sentimental on us—just keep your adoration of one another to yourselves like good polite people. It isn't anything new, you know. We've all been in love.

ZULAL. If I could be in love again, just the same, I think the surprise of it would be beyond saying. I have come near now and then over the past twenty or more years, but near is no better than far, it is the same. Still, still, I remember the few times when I was in love, and oh, how I wish it could happen again. I suppose you mean we are the luckiest people in the world because we are Armenians, is that right, Hrachia, of Erevan?

HRACHIA. Of course it is right, but it is not what I have in mind, not entirely at any rate, for if the truth is told, and I am sure we have all read it in at least two or three books by two or three writers, everybody is Armenian, is that not so, Saroyan, did you not say so somewhere?

SAROYAN. Oh, yes, I did, but I was informed that a Jewish writer had said the same thing a year or two before I had done so—or was it a month or two. He said and how right he was: Everybody is a Jew. In other words, everybody is everybody else, and if that has no scientific merit, it certainly does not have any kind of demerit. It is a fact. Tell us why, Hrachia.

HRACHIA. Very simple. We are the luckiest people in the world because we are here, in this editorial office, talking, which means we are breathing and alive, and incidentally Armenians.

STEPAN. Please understand that in ceasing to listen, and to be a witness to our presence here, and to again resume speaking, I have not intended to deliver a sermon, a preachment, for any who have heard me at the church on Jean Goujon knows that I can do everything in our fine ritual, but when it comes to opening my mouth with a message for the congregation I make a shambles of it, so that even while I speak I ask myself why did I go into the church, was it laziness, was I afraid to open a grocery store, or to study law, or medicine, or to become a buyer and seller of rugs, and may Heaven forgive me, this is the kind of thing a man of the church ought to keep to himself, but I handed it over to you, because I must, you must understand that what I am about to say is not as a man of the church but as a man, an Armenian.

ZULAL.   Well, yes, go ahead, after that long introduction I for one can't wait to know what your pronouncement is, or is the introduction more important than the pronouncement? Make the pronouncement, please.

STEPAN.   Our trouble as a people is that we are all of us individuals, and we cannot permit ourselves to form any kind of a collective, and that of course is the basis of all nations, all governments, all societies. The church would not agree with me in this pronouncement, but I'm afraid that here and now I have no choice but to make it. That is the pronouncement.

ZULAL.   It is the same pronouncement I have heard about us all my life.

ARPIK.   There is very nearly no piece of writing that comes to this editorial office that does not contain that pronouncement in one form or another—as long as I can remember. Father, if I may put it that way, Stepan, friend, where have you been? Surely you did not imagine that you had come upon this thought all by yourself and had not heard it all your life, both in and out of the confines of the church and the schools you attended to become a bishop. Do you expect us to believe what you just said? If so, then I believe, but I must say I find it very strange.

STEPAN.   Oh, of course I heard, and I still hear, but how shall I put it, just now I believed I was making a pronouncement that goes beyond what I had heard, what we have all heard, and I am left deeply embarrassed.

HRACHIA.   Well, don't be, don't be at all, there is more to your pronouncement than the words you put it in, for if you were a poet by trade and experience you might have put it in the one way which would carry the meaning I know you believe the pronouncement really has. Your pronouncement, churchman, is actually a very Christian question, and very simple, although the answer to it is not simple at all. Your pronouncement actually asks why are we unable and unwilling to form any kind of collective or society or culture or government, and the answer is this, believe me, I have not had that much to drink, the answer is that in the very business of failing to form a collective we form a collective, we have always been held tightly together as Armenians by our diversity, by our individuality, by our seeming refusal to line ourselves up like soldiers in an army, to take orders from captains, to speak in one voice, to...would you pour a little here, please? I have just come from Erevan, and I know almost everybody believes we are under the thumb of both the government in Moscow and our own government, and that our individuality is blurred to the point of total effacement, and that the way we are obliged to be Armenians in Soviet Armenia is not the way any Armenian in the Dispersion is willing to believe is the right way, but let me tell you something, believers and disbelievers alike, the bishop has spoken well, his pronouncement is not the same as the pronouncement we have all heard all our lives, it is a new pronouncement, and what he is saying is something I also want to say, and with all my heart: For God's sake, accept with intelligence, accept with gladness, accept with gratitude, accept with Armenian depth of understanding our good fortune to have Moscow, Russian, Communism, Leninism, Marxism, Socialism, collectivisation and all the rest of it to keep us who we are, and to permit us to grow as fully as we are able.

BITLIS.   I say to you Hrachia may you live long, that is the holy truth.

STEPAN.   Holy? That's my department. Well, thank you, Hrachia, and who now is willing to say that my pronouncement is not a pronouncement?

ZULAL.   I am. If we are Armenians at all it is always because we have refused to be neutralised by any order of force or intimidation, and we are refusing right here and now.

ANOUSHAVAN.   Oh. I'm sorry, I did not know you were having a meeting.

ARPIK.   No, no, don't go, Anoushavan, this is not a meeting, it is only a spontaneous Armenian *hunjook*, or entertainment out of ourselves, for ourselves, with amusement, even with loud laughter. For as you see we are pouring whiskey and drinking. Khachig please pour our old friend Anoushavan Kapikian a nice drink. I will say only his name, and anybody who is a stranger to him can make the necessary explanation of who he is.

SAROYAN. Well, what would the explanation be?

ARPIK. The answers to the questions you are always asking. Your name, your city, not in the Diaspora but in Armenia, your profession, your age, your party affiliation, and God knows what else you might suddenly decide to ask another Armenian.

SAROYAN. I have never asked anybody: Are you happy? And I mention this not because I presume that nobody is or that Armenians are certainly at least happy to be Armenians, but because American people are always asking that question, and of course it is a piece of simple absurdity. It is embarrassing to hear, to refuse to hear, to pretend not to hear, to try to take seriously, to try to answer, and to try to speak of something else. The asking of that question is the favorite American piece of bad manners, and the New York crowd insists on asking it all the time. I may ask a lot of questions of Armenians, but I have never asked that one.

ARPIK. Well, thanks, but if you had asked it, I believe I might have been happy to remark, Yes, thank you, I am happy, and then of course I would say to myself, Where did this fool come from? Surely he knows that nobody in the world is happy, or needs to be, let alone an Armenian.

SAROYAN. I don't disagree with that, at all, but I do find that becoming acquainted with myself as the years go by, or as my very limited experience and knowledge informs me of it, that I am quite pleased in a comfortable way to know that my unhappiness is the same as my happiness would be, if you know what I mean, and it doesn't matter, you don't have to know. The idea is that I find it desirable in meeting new people to somewhat know who they are, and if they happen to be Armenians, then I like to hear their names clearly, and their city or village, or that of their people, their fathers or grandfathers. So many Armenians have never set foot in Armenia, either Soviet, or the lost lands, but I did get to Bitlis a good thirteen or fourteen years ago.

BITLIS. I read all about it in *Marmara* at the time, written by your traveling companion Bedros Zobian, the editor of *Marmara*. We all believed you yourself would write about that visit to Bitlis, but so far we have not seen or heard of any such writing. Why did you not write about your return to Bitlis—for it was a return, even though you were born in Fresno, California.

ARPIK. The man from Pasadena, he hates Frezzzno. He thinks Pasadena is the place to be. Why didn't you write about your return to Bitlis?

SAROYAN. Well, there was only one Armenian in Bitlis, the rest were Kurds, and I told them that they seemed to be not only Armenians but that they were Saroyans or Garoghlanians, and on top of the fort a Kurdish *ashough* sang improvised songs about my visit to beautiful Bitlis. Well, when I got back to Fresno I didn't know where to start, and in the end the only thing I wrote was a kind of poem called Bitlis, but it does not really tell what is in my heart to tell, which I don't really know how to tell, for the old Armenian only asked us to please get him to Beirut so that he could die among Armenians. He had been born in Bitlis, he was nearly ninety years old, he was mocked as an old man by the young wild Kurdish kids, and as you know the Armenians also, kids and adults both, have this strange ability to mock the disadvantaged and lonely and lost and helpless. That old Armenian became to me all of us driven out of Bitlis, and yet I was not at all unfond, I hope you understand, of the lively ill-mannered Kurds living in our fine stone houses. It is a very difficult thing to make sense of loss, and absence, and displacement, and destruction—but whoever is alive in a place, he is the owner of the place, that is the law of history, and Bitlis is gone, and I wish I knew how it might be brought back to us.

KHACHIG. Only by fighting for it.

HRACHIA. Spoken like a Dashnak, a revolutionary, but of the year 1895. No, there are other ways.

ZULAL. What are we talking about? Is it poetry? Or is it politics? I mean, what is it that has real meaning for each of us? Isn't it what we keep deepest inside, unconditionally ours, and not what gets itself forever entangled in politics, geography, history, race, religion, language, and back again to politics. Gostandian turned his back on everything but poetry and went up into the wilderness above Marseilles and lived his own private life, and wrote his poems. What are we really talking about?

HRACHIA. And why? Perhaps the question needs to be made a little fuller, Zulal. Let us not forget that I am both a reader of poems and a writer of them, and even politics, as you put it with a touch of scorn, is necessary, absolutely necessary, even for lyric poetry-writing, even for the writing of love poems, so let us deepen the question. We are talking about one thing and this one thing somehow embraces all others.

KHACHIG. And just what thing is that?

HRACHIA. Being who we are, that's what. If we deny it, if we run away from it, we become more who we are, but dismally so, desperately so, and we become sick, don't we? Your friend turned his back on what, pray tell? On himself, on his father and his father's father, and his mother and his mother's mother. I know his poems, I like his poems, but I wish to God he had written them out of being who he was and not out of some fantasy of rejection and re-discovery of himself. Who is it that any of us can discover in the first place, reject, and re-discover? It is always not even himself, if the truth is told, it is his family, his race, his tribe, his history, his geography, his religion, his language, and all of the other things that Zulal brought back to mind. Is this merely Hrachia, this fat man addicted to whiskey and talk, or is it something and somebody more and better? Well, it it is something more, the more must be in the depth of the tribe and history, and if it is something better it must be in the language by means of which we find out, each of us, his reality, both natural and artful. I wrote a poem last year, when my weight was the greatest it has evey been, and in that poem I was the slim eager Armenian boy I had been in Erevan when I was eighteen, and I thanked my father and my mother and all of my ancestors, and our geography, and all the rest of it.

KHACHIG. Recite that poem, please, for it must be something.

ZULAL. Don't do it, Hrachia, please don't do it, you will only embarrass yourself. I know how it is when we are having alcohol, we believe our writing of this or that is truly great, at last, but if we recite it and others hear us they look at one another and ask, Is the man drunk? Has he lost his mind? The poem is not only ordinary, it is badly written. Please, for the sake of your father and mother, for the sake of yourself, for your fat self, if you like, for the sake of all of us, Armenians everywhere, don't recite it, let us imagine that it is indeed precisely as you say it is, and let us not know, let us never know, what it really is, for as long as we are not sure that it is really nothing there is a chance that it is indeed something, and we can think we are all of us companions of the poet who wrote it and of all poets who have written all of the poems that mean more to us than we ourselves sometimes mean to ourselves. I mean, right now, do you know what I am thinking my friend, Hrachia? I am thinking that if the poem you wrote last year is not precisely as you say it was, I don't want to live, that's all. And I can't risk having you recite it, for if I find it less than you said, less than I believe it ought to be, I will quickly leave this pleasant if troublesome place, this gathering together by accident of a variety of us, and go wander into the streets trying to decide how I am either to become dead, or what excuse I am to give myself this time that I must, I must somehow continue to go on living. And I am running out of excuses.

ARPIK. Dear heart, I have always said that you are a romantic young man, and so you are, so you are, let him recite his great poem.

KHACHIG. No, let him not.

HRACHIA. I can't, in any case. Unlike most poets I have no ability for committing my writing to memory, and the manuscript is in Erevan, thank God. I don't want Zulal to be troubled by my writing, or by his own, or by the poems of Keats or Byron or Shelley. I am troubled only by the great poems of our own poets.

ZULAL. Well, as far as I am concerned the reason I like Keats is that he is Armenian, and his feelings are ours.

SYLVIA. Are we dying? Is that the reason this haphazard gathering and our accidental remarks to one another seem somehow so much more really meaningful to us—to me, at any rate—than they can possibly be, and I keep asking myself why is this. Is it because as Armenians each of us is different from all of the others, each of us is profoundly isolated from the others, each with his secrets, terrible and yet also somehow grand, and always Armenian, how or why is beyond me, each of us himself and yet Armenian? Are we hanging onto this disorganized get-together as if it is a matter of life and death, not just for each of us, but for Armenians and Armenia itself, and for all I know for all nations and all nationalities?

ARPIK. You are the youngest person here, Sylvia, and you and I are the only women, and yet it is you, and nobody old, such as, oh, any of these others, who somehow has either felt what you are feeling, or if any of them have felt it, none of them has spoken of it. Well, how does it happen, gentlemen, old friends, new friends, that this dark pretty Armenian girl who is in love, how does it happen that she and not any of you has noticed the special character of this meeting?

ZOHRAB.   Youth feels the end far more sharply than age. The healthy
person understands and imagines disease far more profoundly than
somebody old and sick. It is as simple as that, but the fact is that
I have felt something like what Sylvia has spoken of, only my feeling
has been more as if somehow our holding fast to this accidental
and spontaneous meeting is in celebration of something—and it seems
to me that we seldom celebrate dying. We honor death and our dead,
but in the midst of life and among the living, however near some
of them may be to the end, and who can say for sure who will go
first, perhaps it will be me, perhaps it will be somebody older, and
perhaps somebody younger, there is no telling, in the midst of being,
of being here, in this world, in this great city, Paris, in this editorial
office of this famous Armenian daily, *Haratch*, it seems to me that
we are not dying, we are celebrating our immortality. It seems to
me, in other words, that I really need not fear death—and I have
feared it, believe me, I have feared it desperately—I need not be
reluctant, even, to accept it with warmth, because we are alive
everywhere, in the Dispersion, in our beloved Soviet Armenia, in
our households, which are not really very much like other
households, in our kitchens and at our tables, in our parlors and
among our paintings and drawings on the walls, and near our pianos
and our violins, we continue to be who we are, and gladly, and
without hatred for anybody, for shall they also not one by one suffer
both knowing and departing? We are not the only human family,
but we are the family that we are, and all of our talk here is out
of that condition of being a family. Yes, I do indeed feel that this
is some kind of very special occasion, and I am trying to decide
if it might have happened somewhere else. Could it, could it happen
in a home, at a table, in the church, or the church garden, after
services, in a shop, at a concert, could it?

HRACHIA.   Of course not, for this is this, and whatever might happen
in the other places, old friend Zohrab, it would have to be different
from this, and very different, for we are a hodgepodge of souls,
of people, one of us very fat, myself, one of us saved from death
by long surgery, yourself, Zohrab, and all of us just off the street,
as it were, not come here as if summoned by law or nature or history
to see one another again, but entirely by means of accident, or
mystery. I am delighted that I came here, for if the truth is told,
being fat this way, I was tempted to put off this visit until tomorrow

and to go to my room with the tailor, also slightly fat, but not fat like this, and have a very nice afternoon sleep. I love to sleep, it is disgraceful, it is terrible, it is surely not an Armenian thing at all.

ZULAL.   No, no, sleep is very Armenian, and while we are at it, let us also notice that it is very Armenian to listen carefully to everything we say in meeting, at a gathering like this—but the truth is that we are all really only enjoying being home, in a sense, for Armenians are never so at home as when they are in an editorial office and near printing presses. Whenever I am most confused about who I am I go in the back and look at the four different black printing presses. I just look at them. What great faces and bodies they have, and what glorious work they are able to do. Go ahead, go ahead, Khachig, are we dying, are we living, are we?

KHACHIG.   You said it, dying, and living, of course.

ZULAL.   My name is Zulal.

ARPIK.   What's that mean?

ZULAL.   Who knows?

ARPIK.   Very well. My name is Arpik.

ZULAL.   I am an architect.

ARPIK.   Very well again. I am the editor of *Haratch*.

ZULAL.   I also teach Armenian literature at the famous Murad School.

ARPIK.   I also attend all Armenian events of political and cultural significance in order to write about them for *Haratch*.

STEPAN.   You also attend religious events.

ARPIK.   Religion is part of culture, but if it is not, that is quite true. I may not attend church services every Sunday, but I do indeed try to get to every large ecclesiastical event at our church on Jean Goujon. And so let us proceed with Zulal's game. Perhaps there is something to it.

ZOHRAB.   My name is Zohrab. I was born in Moush. I nearly died in Paris.

BITLIS.   My name is Dikran. I was born in Bitlis. I have never died, or nearly died, but I have lived so long that I know I must soon die.

KHACHIG.   Alas, may that day be far in the future. My name is Khachig. I was born in Aleppo.

SYLVIA.   My name is Sylvia. I was born in Worcester.

STEPAN.   My name is Stephan. I was born in Jerusalem.

ANOUSHAVAN.   My name is Anoushavan. I was born in Gultik, a village near Bitlis. Long live Armenia.

ARPIK. Why did you say that? Nobody else said any such thing.

ANOUSHAVAN. I don't know why. I had to say it.

ARPIK. An Armenian daily paper is not easy to get out year after year.

ZULAL. I read poetry in two or three languages, but really enjoy reading it in Armenian, even including poetry translated from English, Italian, French, German, Russian, and so on and so forth. Saroyan?

SAROYAN. My name is William. I was born in Fresno, my people were born in Bitlis. I am writing a play.

HRACHIA. About what?

ZULAL. You are not abiding by the rules.

HRACHIA. Very well. My name is Hrachia. I was born in Van. What is your play about, Saroyan.?

SAROYAN. Us, of course. Armenians.

HRACHIA. Yes, yes, but tell us more, what happens, who are the characters?

SAROYAN. Us, of course, again. I am also thinking.

HRACHIA. When? Now? What are you thinking?

SAROYAN. I am always thinking. When I am fast asleep I am not fast asleep, I am actually in deep thought, thinking and thinking.

HRACHIA. Saroyan, we are friends these many years, thank God, but what are you thinking and thinking?

SAROYAN. I don't know, I am thinking something, and then I am thinking something else.

KHACHIG. I also teach English and American literature at a college. By saying you are always thinking it doesn't tell us very much now, does it? So what do you mean? Surely you mean something, and you are a writer these many years, so you know how to express yourself, so what do you mean?

SAROYAN. I am thinking everything.

ZOHRAB. Not nothing. I am always thinking nothing.

SAROYAN. I am most thinking everything when I am thinking nothing, it is not possible really to think nothing and not at the same time to think everything.

HRACHIA. Saroyan, I believe you are telling us something, but what is it? I listen and listen and all I hear is that you are thinking and thinking, but there is surely more to it than that, so what is it?

SAROYAN.   Who shall remember us if we don't? Who shall remember the Armenians if they don't remember themselves?

HRACHIA.   Ah, that's it, that is what you are thinking. I thought so. And you are right, you are right again. Who, who, if not us.

ARPIK.   How, though, how shall we remember ourselves?

HRACHIA.   As we are, as we really and truly are, of course. Like this.

ARPIK.   Meeting and talking?

SAROYAN.   And being there. Somewhere. As here. As now.

ARPIK.   Stepan, you seem to be lost in thought, and for a man of the church that amounts to being sick, or on the verge of doubt—what is it?

STEPAN.   No, no, not at all, Arpik, I am not sick, I am not on the verge of doubt—don't you know that the greater the churchman the greater his struggle with doubt? Even our beloved Vasken has several times replied to writers from all over the world about this matter of doubt: it is always there, it is a constant, it is not a temporary condition, it is everlasting, the same as belief, so of course even if I were on the verge of doubt, as you put it, I would not be in a strange country of the mind and spirit, doubt is part of faith and a very powerful part of it. And as for my being lost in thought— well, yes, that is so. I keep thinking, now, where are we? Now. Now. Now where? Now where are we? For it does seem to me that this is a continuation of something that happened before, and also is happening all the time, everywhere, or at any rate wherever there are Armenians spread about in a town or city, who now and then, by accident, find themselves together in a place, but altogether without a plan or purpose. I seem to be thinking, Why is this happening this way? Why doesn't anybody discover that he must go home, or go somewhere else? That may be the thought that you believe you saw in my face, Arpik. I don't know. I did not intend to stay longer than a moment, but now I do not want to go. Was it so with you, Hrachia, when you came here?

HRACHIA.   Well, I had hoped to receive a glass of whiskey, yes, and then to move along. I have many places I must visit, it is always so, coming from Erevan there are chores to attend to, people to see and speak with, but yes, you are quite right, I did not expect to stay this long. But it isn't the good whiskey alone that keeps me, it is, as you have said, ourselves, but here somehow suddenly more than ourselves, each of us more than himself. Is that not so, Saroyan?

SAROYAN.   If you say so, it is so. Yes.

SELECTED BIBLIOGRAPHY

Only those works cited or used in the Introduction, text, and Glossary of this book are listed below.

Unpublished Works of William Saroyan

(Copies of typescripts belonging to the William Saroyan Foundation are in the William Saroyan Archive, Bancroft Library, University of California, Berkeley)

"All about Armenians," a book.
"An Imaginary Character Named Saroyan," a play.
"Bitlis," a book.
"Dreams of Reality," a play.
"Fifty-Fifty," a long memoir.
"Growing Up in Fresno," a radio interview on KPFA and KFCF, Pacifica Radio in Berkeley and Fresno, on February 17, 1976; a transcript was prepared by the Fresno Free College Foundation.
"Home to Hayastan," a play.
"Is There Going to Be A Wedding?" a play.
"Mihr," a play.
"Ouzenk, Chouzenk, Hai Yenk," a play "to be performed in Armenian."
"Tales of the Vienna Streets," a play.
"The Armenian Play or Opera," a play or opera.
"The Human Head," a play.
"The Istanbul Comedy," a play.
"The Jew," a play.
"The Moscow Comedy," a play.
"The Saroyans," a play.
"Turks in the World," a play.
"Warsaw Visitor," a play.

Published Works of William Saroyan

"Antranik of Armenia," *Inhale & Exhale*. New York: Random House, 1936.
Assassinations & Jim, Sam & Anna: Two Short Paris Summertime Plays of 1974. Northridge, California: The Santa Susana Press, 1979.

Births. Berkeley: Creative Arts Book Company, 1983.

"Bitlis," *Ararat*, vol. 25, no. 2 (Spring, 1984), 18-22.

"Candid Conversation: an Interview with Saroyan," conducted in Paris, May 25, 1975 by Garig Basmadjian, *Ararat*, vol. 25, no. 2 (Spring, 1984), 35-46.

"Getztze *Haratch* (Long Live *Haratch*)," *Haratch 50*, Paris, 1976, 383-84, in English with Armenian title.

"Hayastan and Charentz," published June 10, 1954 in the *Hairenik Weekly*, reprinted as "Armenia and Her Poet Charentz," in *I Used to Believe I Had Forever, Now I'm Not So Sure*, and most recently in *My Name Is Saroyan*.

Here Comes, There Goes, You Know Who. New York: Simon and Schuster, 1961.

Inhale & Exhale. New York: Random House, 1936.

I Used to Believe I Had Forever, Now I'm Not So Sure. New York: Cowless, 1968.

Letters From 74 rue Taitbout or Don't Go, But If You Must, Say Hello to Everybody. New York: World Publishing Company, 1969.

My Name Is Aram. New York: Harcourt, Brace and Company, 1940.

My Name Is Saroyan, compiled with a commentary by James H. Tashjian. New York: Coward-McCann, Inc., 1983.

Obituaries. Berkeley: Creative Arts Book Company, 1979.

"104 Unpublished Letters of William Saroyan: Ethnic Motivations of an American Writer," edited with a commentary by James H. Tashjian, *The Armenian Review*, vol. 34, no. 3 (September, 1981), Saroyan Memorial Issue.

Places Where I've Done Time. New York: Praeger Publishers, 1972.

Rock Wagram. Garden City, New York: Doubleday & Company, 1951.

Sam, the Highest Jumper of Them All or The London Comedy. London: Faber and Faber, 1961.

Sons Come and Go, Mothers Hang in Forever. New York: McGraw-Hill, 1976.

"Sunday Is a Hell of a Day," *The American Mercury* (August, 1957), reprinted in *I Used to Believe I Had Forever, Now I'm Not So Sure*.

The Daring Young Man on the Flying Trapeze and Other Stories. Deluxe limited edition reprint of the work of 1934. Covelo, California: Yolla Bolla Press, 1984.

The Dogs, or The Paris Comedy and Two Other Plays. New York: Phaedra, 1969.

"The First Armenian Presbyterian Church, Fresno, 1919," in *Places Where I've Done Time*, 170-71.

The Human Comedy. New York: Harcourt, Brace and Company, 1943.

"The Man Who Knew My Father as a Boy in Bitlis," *Hairenik Weekly*, February 25, 1942, reprinted in *My Name Is Saroyan*.

The Man with His Heart in the Highlands and Other Stories. New York: Dell, 1968.

The New Saroyan Reader, A Connoisseur's Anthology of the Writings of William Saroyan, compiled by Brian Darwent. Berkeley: Creative Arts Book Company, 1984.

"The Santa Fe Depot, Fresno, 1922," in *Places Where I've Done Time*.

The Time of Your Life. New York: Harcourt, Brace and Company, 1939.

Tracy's Tiger. Garden City, New York: Doubleday & Company, 1951.

Books and Articles about William Saroyan

Arlen, Michael J. *Passage to Ararat.* New York: Farrar, Straus & Giroux, 1975.

Calonne, David Stephen. *William Saroyan, My Real Work Is Being.* Preface by Dickran Kouymjian. Chapel Hill: The University of North Carolina Press, 1983.

Curtiss, Thomas Quinn. "Saroyan's 'Tales' Due for Vienna Premiere." *International Herald Tribune*, July 31, 1981.

Floan, Howard. *William Saroyan.* New York: Twayne, 1966.

Hamalian, Leo, ed. "A Special Issue on William Saroyan," *Ararat*, vol. 25, no. 2 (Spring, 1984).

Knapp, Grace H. *The Tragedy of Bitlis.* New York: Flemming H. Rivett Company, 1919.

Kouymjian, Dickran. "A Note on the Background of *Haratch* and Saroyan's Writing Techniques." *William Saroyan Festival Program*

November 2-22, 1981, Fresno: California State University, 1981, 12-13.

_____, "Saroyan and *Haratch* or William Saroyan's Last Armenian Play," *Haratch*, monthly literary supplement (July, 1981), 2-4, in Armenian.

_____, "Saroyan on the Armenians: *Haratch* and other Unpublished Plays," *William Saroyan Festival Program*. Fresno: California State University, 1981, 3-11.

_____, "The Last of the Armenian Plays." *Ararat*, vol. 25, no. 2 (Spring, 1984), 24-27.

_____, "William Saroyan et l'expérience ethnique arménienne." *Arménia*, no. 88 (December, 1984), 48-51.

Lee, Lawrence and Barry Gifford. *Saroyan, A Biography*. New York: Harper & Row, 1984.

Samuelian, Varaz. *Willie and Varaz: Memories of My Friend William Saroyan*. Fresno: Panorama West Books, 1985.

Saroyan, Aram. *Last Rites: The Death of William Saroyan*. New York: William Morrow and Company, 1982.

_____, *William Saroyan*. New York: Harcourt, Brace and Jovanovich, 1983.

GLOSSARY

(Characters in the plays are usually listed under their first names.)

Abkhazia, Abkhazian, autonomous region of the Georgian Soviet Socialist Republic with coastline on the Black Sea.

Agamian, tailor in *Haratch* at whose home Hrachia was staying; probably Etvart (Edward) Aghamian, tailor and poet originally from Istanbul. He was Secretary of the Armenian Writers Union of France for some years, but repatriated to Soviet Armenia 1974 or 1975 where he later died. His apartment was on Rue Chateaudun, around the corner from Saroyan's Rue Taitbout dwelling. Krikor Atamian (1904-1985) was also a tailor and close friend of Saroyan's with a shop in the same neighborhood on Rue Lafayette.

Agri, formerly Karakilise, last major town on the main highway toward Mount Ararat in eastern Turkey.

Akhmed, Arabic name, modern Turkish *Ahmet*, Turkish owner of restaurant in Bitlis; Saroyan's phonetic spelling was "Ahkhmed."

Akop Dudu, dudu in dialectical Armenian means elderly woman of respect; modern Turkish retains the word with the meaning "elderly Armenian woman." Akop is a form of Hakob, western Armenian Hagop, the biblical equivalent of Jacob.

Ali, a Turkish photographer, one of three who covered Saroyan's trip to Bitlis in 1964.

Almast, octogenarian woman, survivor of the Genocide and helper of Fr. Kasparian at Holy Trinity in the play *Haratch*. Her name means diamond in Persian.

Anadole, Anatolia, the Turkish form is more exactly "Anadolu."

Anoushavan, see Kapikian and Vashpazian.

Antranik Ozanian, General (1865-1927), the most celebrated Armenian military figure of modern times, symbol of Armenia's resistance to the Turk and the revolutionary struggle for independence. Appointed commander in 1915 of the First Armenian Legion of volunteers on the Russian-Persian front. Forced by the British in 1919 to give up military activities, he left the Caucasus for London and Paris to plead the Armenian cause; rebuffed and discouraged, he settled in Fresno in 1922 and died there in 1927 on August 30, a day before Saroyan's ninth birthday. His body was shipped to Soviet Armenia, but was not accepted, resulting in burial in Père-Lachaise cemetery in Paris. Saroyan had a special attraction to Antranik; see his "Antranik of Armenia" in *Inhale & Exhale*. He frequently visited the monument erected at Antranik's grave site.

Ara Altounian, an Armenian from Istanbul who accompanied Saroyan on his 1964 trip to Bitlis. Altounian, though trained as a dentist, apparently never practised but rather turned to business and industry. The trio drove to Bitlis in Altounian's 1958 Chevrolet.

arak, see *rakhi*.

Arakelian, Krikor (1871-1957), the watermelon king of California and the founder of Mission Bell Wine; see Saroyan's "The Santa Fe Depot, Fresno, 1922," in *Places Where I've Done Time*, pp.24-25, for background.

Aram Saroyan, brother of Saroyan's maternal grandmother, Lucintak Garoghlanian Saroyan.

Ardahan, name of city and province now in northeastern Turkey, but between 1918-1920 part of the Independent Republic of Armenia.

Arlen, Michael J., staff writer on the *New Yorker* magazine and author of *Passage to Ararat*; his father, novelist Michael Arlen (1895-1956), was a friend of Saroyan.

Armenak Saroyan (born in Bitlis, 1874—died in Campbell, California, 1911), was William Saroyan's father. Though he died of a ruptured appendix when Saroyan was a child, William cherished his memory tenaciously. He left some writings in English and Armenian that have never been published. Under the influence of Protestant missionaries in Bitlis he became an ordained minister, with his first congregation in Paterson, New Jersey, and a second in Yettem, California, which he gave up for chicken farming.

Armenian Republic, declared on May 28, 1918, almost simultaneously with the independent Georgian and Azerbaijani Republics; it became sovietized, like the others, in late 1920. It was the first independent Armenian state since the fall of the Armenian kingdom of Cilicia in 1375. The Dashnak Party swept its elections and controlled the state; thus it is often referred to as the Dashnak Republic.

Arpik, see Missakian, Arpik.

Asbarez, the Armenian newspaper "Arena," founded in Fresno in 1908 and transferred to Los Angeles in 1974. It is an organ of the Dashnak Party. Its office, on Ventura opposite the Holy Trinity Armenian Church, was called the Patriotic Club in *Armenians*.

ashough, Armenian for troubadour or minstrel; Saroyan spelled it *ahshkhukh* in the typescript of *Haratch*.

Azerbaijan, Azerbaijanian, Azerbaijani Soviet Socialist Republic is, along with Armenia and Georgia, one of the three Caucasian Republics. Saroyan used the spelling "Aizairbajanians." The Azerbaijanis are Muslim Turks; their language is called Azeri.

bagharsh, in Armenian more correctly *bagharch*; literally "unleavened bread." Saroyan's typescript has *bahghahrch*.

Baghesh, see Bitlis.

Barzani, an important Kurdish tribe.

bashban, corruption of Armenian *"bashtban,"* protector or defender.

Bedros Saroyan, paternal grandfather of Saroyan.

Bedros Zobian (Zobyan), the Armenian who arranged Saroyan's trip to Bitlis in 1964 was an architect by profession. In 1958 he inherited the responsibility of publishing the Armenian daily *Marmara* after the death of its editor Souren Shamlian, Zobian's father-in-law. Bedros and his wife Seta shared editorial responsibilities of *Marmara* until their resettlement in Canada in 1967. The Zobians visited Saroyan in Fresno in that same year. They are still proprietors of the paper.

Bitlis, Armenian Baghesh, ancient Armenian center west of Lake Van; important in the medieval and modern period. The mountain city is today inhabited by Kurds who began settling in the city after the fifteenth century and simply appropriated the whole place after the Armenians were driven out and massacred in 1915.

Bitlistsi or *Bitlistzi*, someone of or from Bitlis.

Bolis, Constantinopolis, the modern Istanbul; the term used in Armenian after the Byzantine Greek Polis ("city") with the consonantal change p to b in modern western Armenian; hence, *Bolsetsi*, one from Constantinople.

Boshbazmanian, Dikran, the eighty-eight year old writer of memoirs from Bitlis in *Haratch*; his real name was Mesrob Ter-Krikorian. He passed away in the early 1980s.

Bourdj Hammoud, an almost exclusively Armenian quarter of Beirut, Lebanon.

bulghour pilaf, *bulghour* is cracked wheat, pilaf a generic term for a Middle Eastern rice dish; the modern Turkish is *bulgur*.

Cahan, Abraham (1860-1951), a founder and editor from 1903 to 1951 of the *Jewish Daily Forward* of New York.

Chilingirian, see Darbinian.

Circassians, northwest Caucasian Muslim people found throughout Anatolia after nineteenth-century migrations.

Committee for Cultural Relations with Armenians Abroad, known better by its Armenian name SPIURK (Diaspora), a most powerful organization through which important Armenians living abroad are invited to Armenia, was established in 1964.

Cosette Saroyan, the oldest of William's sisters was born in 1899; she resides in San Francisco in the house Saroyan had built for her and his mother in 1939.

Darbinian, Reuben (1882-1968), Armenian revolutionary intellectual of the Dashnak Party, Minister of Justice of the Armenian Republic in 1920, and editor of the *Hairenik Daily* in Boston starting in 1922; he began publishing Saroyan stories and poems in 1933 before the great success of the author. Saroyan admired him and in 1968 dedicated a collection of stories to him: *The Man with His Heart in the Highlands and Other Stories*; see J. Tashjian, *Armenian Review*, vol. XXXIV, no. 3 (1981) and *My Name Is Saroyan* on their relationship.

Dashnak, also Tashnag in western Armenian, the short name for the Armenian Revolutionary Federation founded in 1890 in Tiflis, Georgia. The party won control of the Armenian Republic of 1918-1920; it also sponsored revolutionary guerilla units to fight against Ottoman Turkish oppression. It is the largest Armenian political party in the diaspora with a network of newspapers and social, cultural,and charitable societies attached to it.

Der Havasarian, Giragos Arpiar, rug merchant in *Armenians*; identity unknown, probably invented by Saroyan.

Dikran, see Boshbazmanian, Dikran.

Dikran Saroyan, a brother of Saroyan's maternal grandmother, Lucintak Garoghlanian Saroyan.

Dikranagert, the city of Diyarbakir, modern Turkish Diyarbekir; the Armenian form comes from the Greek Tigranocerta, the famous capital of the greatest of Armenian kings, Tigran/Dikran the Great, built in the first century B.C. in the general vicinity of the modern town.

Erevan, also *Yerevan*, with the Russian form *Erivan*; the capital of the Soviet Republic of Armenia with a present population of 1,300,000; before World War I it was a small, dusty provincial capital of 30,000. At that time the major Armenian city was Tiflis, capital of Georgia, with a majority of Armenian inhabitants and, along with Istanbul, the most important intellectual, cultural, and commercial Armenian center.

Erzeroum, the ancient city of Theodosiopolis, Armenian Garin, a major Armenian commercial center for centuries. Very few Armenians from the city survived the massacres of 1915.

Etchmiadzin, the spiritual center of the Armenian church and the seat of the Armenian Catholicos, the supreme pontiff. Founded in the early fourth century by St. Gregory the Illuminator, the word literally means the "Descent of the Only Begotten." It is in the town of Vagharshapat, the former royal capital, about twenty miles from Erevan. Saroyan's phonetic spelling was Aitchmiadzine.

gahdah, Armenian plain cake or brioche, pronounced *kata* by most western Armenian speakers.

Garoghlanian, also *Garaoghlanian, Lucintak*, Saroyan's maternal grandmother whose husband Minas Saroyan died in 1901 in Bitlis. A strong woman who related endless stories and folktales to her grandson. *Gara* or *kara*, means "black" or according to some authorities "brave" in Turkish and *oghlan*, "boy;" thus, son of the dark or brave lad. Saroyan used the more precise Garaoghlanian in *Bitlis*, but the more usual Garoghlanian in *Haratch*. He liked to use the pseudonym Aram Garoghlanian and even listed his Fresno telephone under the name.

Georgia, Georgian, Soviet Socialist Republic of the Caucasus, north of Armenia; its capital, Tiflis, was, in the nineteenth and early twentieth centuries, the most important Armenian city in the east. Georgian is not an Indo-European language like Armenian; the Georgians are Orthodox Christians but of the Byzantine rite. They shared the Bagratid ruling dynasty with Armenia in the medieval period.

giaour, also *giavour*, Turkish for "infidel," especially used for Christians, a very pejorative term banned by Turkish law in 1985. Saroyan used the spelling "gaouir."

Giligia, western Armenian for Cilicia, the southwestern most region of the historical Armenian lands touching the Mediterranean coast. A powerful medieval Armenian kingdom ruled there until 1375.

Giresun, Black Sea port which had a sizable Armenian colony before the Genocide.

Gostandian, Harout (1909-1979), Persian Armenian poet educated in Bombay who settled in a small town in Provence in 1926. Zoulal Kazandjian, a character in *Haratch*, was a great admirer of his.

Gultik, also *Kultik,* more correctly *Ghultik,* a town ten kilometers southeast of Bitlis with some 400 Armenian families before 1915. It has been renamed Aridağ.

Hairenik, in Armenian "fatherland," an association as well as a series of periodicals—daily, weekly, and monthly—headquartered in Boston since the turn of the century but moved to Watertown in 1985. They are the most influential organs of the Dashnak Party. Saroyan published scores of stories and poems in the pages of its various publications starting as early as 1933 under both his own name and the pseudonym "Sirak Goryan." They have been collectively published in *My Name Is Saroyan.*

Hampartzoumian, Victor (born 1908), world famous astrophysicist, head of the Biurakan Observatory in Soviet Armenia, President of the Armenian Academy of Sciences, and member of the Soviet Academy of Sciences.

Haratch, Armenian daily newspaper founded in Paris in 1925 by Schavarch Missakian and now edited by his daughter, Arpik Missakian; it has been the major Armenian daily in Europe.

Harpoot, see Kharpert.

Hayastan, the Armenian word for "Armenia," thus *Hay* means "Armenian."

Hrachia Hovhannissian, Soviet Armenian writer, friend of Saroyan's and editor of *Soviet Grakanoutiwn (Soviet Literature),* a monthly journal published in Erevan.

Hripsime Saroyan, paternal grandmother of William.

hunjook, Armenian "banquet," "feast," "party;" the correct Armenian form is *khnjoyk.*

Issy-les-Moulineaux, southern suburb of Paris with a large Armenian minority and an Armenian church.

Jean Goujon, a Paris street in the eighth arrondissement between the Champs-Elysées and the Seine where in 1913 the Armenian cathedral was built; it is casually referred to as the church of Jean Goujon.

Jewish Daily Forward, the original U.S. Yiddish newspaper founded in New York in 1897 and associated closely with Abraham Cahan (1860-1951), who was its editor from 1903 to 1951.

Jivelekian, Doctor Arshak, character in *Armenians,* where we learn of his education at Harvard and his age, 58. It seems no doctor by that name actually practised in Fresno.

Kapikian, Anoushavan (1898-), a regular at *Haratch* over the years and a custom bootmaker; his brother Khoren is a well-known writer; originally from Shabin Karahissar and not Gultik as in the play.

Kars, important Armenian city lost to the Turks in 1920; the tenth century Armenian church of the Holy Apostles remains the principal landmark in the present Turkish city where no Armenians live.

Kasparian, Father Vartan (Bursa 1874-Los Angeles 1966), resident priest of Holy Trinity Armenian Apostolic Church on Ventura and M Street in Fresno from 1912 to ca. 1932. He was a celibate priest with the rank of *vardapet* (archimandrite) when he came to America from Bursa, where he was assistant prelate. He eventually became Prelate of the Armenian Church in California with the rank of archbishop.

Khachatourian, Aram (1903-1978), most famous Soviet Armenian composer, who in the immediate post-war period was considered among the big three of Soviet composers after Shostakovitch and Prokovief. His Gayane Ballet suite with its famous Sabre Dance was based on Armenian folk melodies.

Khachig, see Tölölyan, Khachig.

Kharpert, sometimes called Harpoot, a former Armenian city in Eastern Anatolia and the capital of an Ottoman sanjak. Its name has been changed to Elazig. There are many Kharperttsies in the United States, some having arrived with the help of Protestant missionaries who were very active there before the Genocide. Apparently a family or two of Armenians still lives there.

Knadjian, Reverend Muggerditch, head of the First Armenian Presbyterian Church of Fresno from 1912 to 1922. Saroyan was fond of him not only because he was a member of his parish, but because Knadjian once brought him some books; see his "First Armenian Presbyterian Church, Fresno, 1919," in *Places Where I've Done Time*.

Krikor Narekatsi, see Narek.

Kuchak, Nahapet (died 1591), famous Armenian secular poet troubadour.

Kurd, ancient Indo-European speaking Muslim people inhabiting Upper Mesopotamia. Today they represent some 10,000,000 in Turkey alone, even though they are not legally recognized as an ethnic group. Turkey refuses to admit the existence of non-Turks, that is minorities, therefore, the Kurds are officially "Mountain Turks," while the Armenians are sometimes referred to as "Christian Turks."

lavash, also *lavush*, Armenian flat bread, often a yard in diameter and paper thin, known also in Armenian as *parag hatz*, thin bread. It is still made by three independent Armenian bakeries in the Fresno area, and is a common feature at all Fresno restaurants.

madzoon or *madzoun*, Armenian word for yogurt.

Malibu, Pacific coast town near Los Angeles where Saroyan had a house in which he lived from 1952 to 1958.

Man from Bitlis, in *Haratch*, see Boshbazmanian, Dikran.

Marmara, an Armenian daily of Istanbul named after the Marmara Sea. It was founded in 1940 by Souren Shamlian. After the latter's death in 1958, the paper has been published by his daughter and son-in-law, Seta and Bedros Zobian.

Marzovan, modern Merzifon, central Anatolian city from which many Armenians migrated to Fresno, including the very earliest settlers of 1881-2. An American missionary college established there was responsible for the educations of hundreds of Armenians prior to the massacres.

Mehmed, Mehmet, Turkish form of Arabic Mahmud, one of the Turkish photographers who covered Saroyan's trip to Bitlis.

Mekhitarist, an Armenian Catholic congregation founded by Mekhitar, an Armenian priest who fled Constantinople in the early eighteenth century, finally settling on the Island of San Lazzaro in the Venice lagoon. The religious order operates schools for Armenian youth throughout the world, including Paris and Los Angeles. A branch of the order was established in Vienna in the nineteenth century.

Minas Saroyan, maternal grandfather of Saroyan, who died in Bitlis in 1901.

Missakian, Arpik (Paris, 1926-), current editor and publisher of *Haratch*, the Armenian daily of Paris. She succeeded her father, Schavarch, in 1957.

Missakian, Schavarch (Sebastia 1886-Paris 1957), Saroyan spelled it Schavarsh to accommodate English pronunciation, founder and editor of *Haratch* daily in Paris in 1925.

Missalonghi, site at the entrance to the Gulf of Corinth of famous naval battles (1821-1826) between the Ottoman Turkish and Greek fleets during the Greek war of independence. Lord Byron died there in 1824.

Moughsi Agha or *Baba,* Armenian *mahtesi*, pilgrim to Jerusalem. Derived Arabic *muqdisi*, someone who has gone to Quds, Arabic for

Jerusalem. The term *haj* or *hajji* is also used for one who has made the pilgrimage. *Baba* is old man or grandfather; *agha*, grandee.

Mountain Turks, a modern and official Turkish government euphemism for the Kurds, a minority of ten million in Turkey.

Moush, Armenian city in the plain of the same name west of Lake Van, and relatively close to Bitlis. There are no Armenians living there today.

Mugo, shortened, familiar form for Armenian Mgrditch, Muggerditch; see Knadjian.

Murad School, College Samuel Moorat, the secondary school of the Mekhitarist fathers in Sèvres, a Paris suburb.

Narek or *Narekatsi, Krikor* (951-1003), Gregory of Narek was one of the most famous Armenian poets of the medieval period, much appreciated for his language and his mystical approach to God.

Otyam, Fikret, Turkish photo-journalist of the popular Istanbul daily *Cumhuriyet* who, along with another Turkish journalist—Haluk Tuncali of the *Daily News* of Istanbul—accompanied Saroyan and his party in a separate jeep on that part of the trip which covered Van, Bitlis, Diyarbekir and Aintab.

Papazian, Reverend Manaseh (Beredjik 1865-1943), pastor of Pilgrim Armenian Congregational Church from 1914 to 1940. After an elaborate education at Yale Divinity (1886-1889) and Andover Theological Seminary, he married the daughter of an important American missionary and with her went to Aintab to serve fifteen years in the Armenian Protestant community. Returning to the United States, he served six and a half years in New York before going to Fresno.

Patriotic Club, the Asbarez Club on Ventura in Fresno. When the paper of the same name moved to Los Angeles in 1974, the meeting place retained its name. Even though a Holiday Inn has taken its place, a new "Patriotic Club" was inaugurated across Ventura and a half a block east from the "Red Brick Church."

peda, also *beda*, a round leavened bread popular among Armenians and Greeks; modern Turkish *pide* refers to a thinner bread.

rakhi, modern Turkish *raki*, Arabic *arak*, a colorless liqueur made from several distillations of grapes with anise flavor; Saroyan's phonetic spelling was *rahkhie* in the typescript of *Armenians*.

Safrastian, Arshak, helped Lucintak Garoghlanian get papers to take the Saroyan family out of Bitlis in 1905; he later lived in London and devoted much of his time to ancient Armenian history. Saroyan met him in England in the 1940s.

Samsun, Black Sea port with an important Armenian colony before 1915.

Samuelian, Hrant (1891-1977), political writer for *Haratch* and founder of the most famous Near Eastern bookstore in Paris, Librairie Orientale Samuelian, still at 51 rue Monsieur-le-Prince in the Latin Quarter; it is now managed by his children, Alice and Armen.

San Lazzaro, an island in the lagoon of Venice given to the Abbot Mekhitar by the Doge in 1722 for the establishment of the Order's monastery. Today, with its chapel, museum, cloisters, and medieval manuscript collection, it remains a place of pilgrimage for Armenians from around the world. See also Mekhitar.

Sarian, Martiros (1880-1972), the most famous Soviet Armenian painter of all time. His portrait of Saroyan is on permanent display in the Sarian House Museum in Erevan.

Sassoun, famous Armenian mountainous region west of Bitlis that resisted Turkish forces during the time of massacres. The people of Sassoun, Sassountsis, are extremely proud of their resistance. The only surviving Armenian folk epic, "David of Sassoun," revolves around the powerful and "crazy" heroes of the area.

scambile, modern Turkish *iskambile*, a popular card game among western or Turkish Armenians.

Shah-Mouradian, Armenak (Moush 1878-Paris 1939), famous singer, a friend of the Armenian composer-musicologist Gomidas/Komitas, whose compositions he gave particularly authentic interpretations. Shah-Mouradian's early recordings were to be found in nearly every Armenian-American home in the 1920s.

shavlar, meaning unknown, Saroyan could have hardly meant *shalvar*, baggy Turkish trousers. It is not clear what word for "fat" he tried to recall in his Program Note for *Armenians*.

Stepan, Bishop, name used in *Haratch* to refer to Archbishop Serovpe Manougian, Primate for the Armenians of Europe until his death in February, 1984. He served in the post for more than twenty years. His only living relative, a niece in Fresno, Abigail Sarkisian, became a close friend of Saroyan. He was not fat as Saroyan has him.

Sylvia Siranoosh Missirlian came to the United States from Beirut as a child, received her B.A. in political science from UCLA and an M.B.A. from Cornell; in 1979 she was twenty-seven years old and a real estate investment analyst. She now resides in San Francisco.

Takoohi Saroyan (Bitlis 1883-4—San Francisco 1950), the mother of William Saroyan, who after more than a year followed her husband Armenak to the United States. Three of her four children were born before their arrival in the U.S. Though she joined her husband on the east coast, she soon persuaded him to move to Fresno where much of her family had already settled. After Armenak's untimely death in 1911, she was forced to put the four children in the Fred Finch Orphanage in Oakland for five years until she could provide for them in Fresno.

Tatvan, a town on the western shore of Lake Van.

Tölölyan, Khachig, now Associate Professor of Comparative Literature teaching at Wesleyan College, Middletown, Connecticut. He arrived in the United States at age sixteen from Aleppo via Beirut. His father Minas was for a long time editor of the *Hairenik Daily* in Boston. He is a prolific writer and critic, and the pages of *Haratch* have welcomed his participation for the past decade.

Trebizond, modern Turkish Trabzon, most famous southern Black Sea port dating back to pre-classical Greek colonial times. Though the Armenian colony was important, it was dwarfed by the Pontic Greek one of the city. Today there are neither Greek nor Armenian inhabitants.

Tsapergor Tagh, a quarter of Bitlis extremely dear to Saroyan because his father's house was there. *Tagh* is Armenian for "quarter." The four quarters of Bitlis were known by their churches: three were named after the Holy Virgin, while the fourth, was called Tsapergor Sourp Garabed (classical Armenian Sourb Karapet), "Holy Precursor," that is St. John the Baptist.

Van, major Armenian city and district (*vilayet* in Turkish) on the lake of the same name in historical Armenia before the Genocide. The historical city is today a desolate field of ruins where once upwards of 25,000 mostly Armenian inhabitants lived; there were about 150,000 Armenians in the *vilayet*. For many it was also one of the major centers of Armenian civilization, having been the royal residence of the Urartian kings in the ninth to the seventh centuries B.C. The Armenians of Van successfully resisted Turkish attack in 1915. Vanetsis have an extremely strong sense of regional pride.

Vashpazian, Anoushavan, according to the "Man from Bitlis" in *Haratch*, the name of an Armenian traitor of the city.

Vasken, a native of Harpoot in the play *Armenians*; the correct classical and eastern or Russian Armenian spelling is Vazgen.

Vasken Vehapar, His Holiness Vazgen I Baldjian (born 1908 in Bucharest, Rumania), was elected Catholicos of All Armenians in 1955 and resides at the Holy See of Etchmiadzin, Soviet Armenia. *Vehapar*, meaning "august," "majestic," is a title reserved for the catholicos. He was a good friend of Saroyan's and held a solemn requiem mass for him in Paris at the Armenian church on Rue Jean Goujon on the first Sunday, May 24, 1981, after the writer's death.

vehapar, see Vasken.

Vy, "alas, oh," common Armenian expression of mild surprise often associated with unpleasant news.

Zhamanak or *Jamanak (Time)*, an Armenian newspaper of Istanbul founded in 1908.

Zohrab, Mouradian (Izmir 1920-), a regular visitor to *Haratch*, a tailor by profession.

Zulal (Zoulal) Kazandjian (Musa Dagh 1936-), architect, poet, critic, and contributor to *Haratch* who also teaches at Samuel Moorat, the Mekhitarist school in Sèvres, a suburb of Paris. Saroyan spelled it Zulal in the English way.